From Christendom
to Freedom

From Christendom to Freedom:
Journey-Making with a Black Transgender Elder

by Jonathon Thunderword

OtherWise Engaged Publishing

First edition April 2020
Cover art by Chris Paige

The bear logo for Jonathon's Trans-Anointing ministry was
designed by Leo Hill. Front cover image of Jonathon provided by
gc2b (gc2b.co) and was illustrated by Farren Koehne for gc2bs
2019 Black History Month campaign titled, "In Full Bloom." Used
with permission. Back cover photograph of Jonathon by Triptta
Cohen-Thunderword. All images used with permission.

ISBN: 978-1-951124-20-5 (Paperback)
ISBN: 978-1-951124-21-2 (Kindle)
eISBN: 978-1-951124-22-9

Published by OtherWise Engaged Publishing
http://otherwiseengaged4u.wordpress.com

Dedicated to Bishop Yvette Flunder
whose sermon "Undressing Jesus"
turned my life around

CONTENTS

Foreword

I first met Jonathon Thunderword in 2005 at a Carl's Junior fast food restaurant while I was in the Navy and stationed in Norfolk, Virginia. My therapist helped me connect with him at a time when my life was falling apart. Thoughts of suicide were my close companions. I was divorced. I had lost my family, friends, financial standing, and church. While my naval career continued, the most intimate parts of my life had fallen away.

Since then, Jonathon has been my best friend, spiritual mentor, and colleague. He has been and continues to be that one person whose integrity I always know that I can trust. At that first meeting, Jonathon and I had a long conversation about life, gender, sexuality, and options for how I might move forward. The uncanny thing is that Jonathon was only back in Norfolk briefly to re-establish By the Way Baptist Church. I was still in the Navy and I would regularly go out to sea for months at a time. There was only a very small window of availability when our paths would have been able to cross—but cross they did!

It was a transgender support group meeting at a club called Nutty Buddy's that helped me find a local therapist who worked with transgender clients. In therapy, I was able to gain some further understanding of my own gender, sexuality, and spirituality, while beginning a journey of liberation from oppressive, even deadly, theological concepts. I also came to understand how gender and sexuality, as expressions of cosmic mystical desire, shape my humanity.

During one therapy session the therapist said, "You're going to be a minister, right?"

I responded, "I think so."

I do not know how this Wiccan therapist figured that out, but her role in my life is a continuing reminder to me that the Divine Imagination, the Spirit of God, works beyond the narrow confines of sectarian religion. Religion, used as a tool of mental, emotional, and spiritual enslavement, is a debilitating structure that regularly denies the voice of the Holy. Yet, my experience of salvation has been profoundly impacted by experiences I have had with Pagan, Wiccan, and Native American practitioners, enabling me to minister with like-minded people of faith to liberate the church from what Jonathon Wilson-Hartgrove, in his book, *Reconstructing the Gospel: Finding Freedom from Slaveholder Religion* (2018), calls the slaveholder religion—so that it might return to the liberating teachings of Jesus of Nazareth, the Christ.

I would go on to attend a local Metropolitan Community Church, which instigated a new imagination, a new horizon, and a new hope in my relationship with the Holy. It was a church where I could bring all of myself authentically. My process of transition was holistic, involving spiritual, physical, and mental dynamics as I bathed in this new experience of grace and mercy. This deep transformation took several years to accomplish— and it was one of the most healing experiences of my entire life.

As a Black man, I had spent years exhausting myself trying to meet the demands and expectations of society. Now that I had failed those standards entirely, both my theological foundations and my identity needed to be rebuilt. I continued in prayer, meditation, and Bible reading in search of authentic communion and a deep oneness with God. Looking back, I see now that grappling with such difficult questions—questions that had no easy answers—was making room for me to deepen my faith while moving toward a more loving, mystical, and grace-filled life.

Indeed, I am now a Christian clergyperson in the Christian Church (Disciples of Christ) and working toward a Doctor of Ministry degree. My call to ministry as a Christian minister of prophetic import could not have happened without these multi-faith influences. I also credit my journey with Jonathon who lovingly helped me to sort them out

In a life that is illuminating, fluid, dynamic, queer, and not easy to define (or even understand), it has been revealed to me that the questions themselves are powerful and transformative—even and perhaps especially when those questions seem terrifying. Meanwhile, the Holy imparts people, places, and things to serve as a comforting reminder that God is journeying with us. I am so very thankful that the Divine Imagination thought to send Jonathon to journey with me through my transition of gender, sexuality, and spirituality. Truly, he has been a persistent reminder of God's presence with me.

One of the many teachings I have gleaned from Jonathon is genuinely to appreciate the people, places, and things that greet me along life's journey. In the midst of those experiences, I have found God's grace and love abundantly. This book is full of such teachings through Jonathon's anecdotes and reflections. It is a book of journey-making—through the complexities of gender and human foibles, from the confines of debilitating religion toward human freedom and liberation. This book is an invitation to experience cosmic desire and the hospitality of the Holy for yourself as you seek oneness with the God of your own understanding.

My spiritual journey has not taken the same shape that Jonathon's has. I did follow him from Norfolk to the Pacific School of Religion to deepen my education, but I remain quite active in Christian community and ministry. I am delighted that you also will have this opportunity—to journey alongside Jonathon while making your own way forward. I invite you to open your heart to new experiences and to claim the freedom and grace to answer your own deepest questions in your own unique way as well. May we all continue to journey together as the Divine invites us into new encounters and new ways of being fully ourselves in this world.

The Reverend Monica Joy Cross
Oakland, California
April 2020

Preface

"Is there anyone here who, planning to build a new house, doesn't first sit down and figure the cost so you'll know if you can complete it? If you only get the foundation laid and then run out of money, you're going to look pretty foolish. Everyone passing by will poke fun at you: 'He started something he couldn't finish.'

"Or can you imagine a king going into battle against another king without first deciding whether it is possible with his ten thousand troops to face the twenty thousand troops of the other? And if he decides he can't, won't he send an emissary and work out a truce?

"Simply put, if you're not willing to take what is dearest to you, whether plans or people, and kiss it good-bye, you can't be my disciple."

Luke 14:28–33
The Message

Sometimes, Christians like to disclose a whole statement of faith upfront. Well, this book is not really for people who might need such a thing. In fact, this book is for people who have struggled to find our place in a world that demands such disclosures. Still, let me share with you some critical turning points from my Christian walk, so you know a little bit about what I have taken from Christian tradition that informs this project (and my life).

Counting the Cost

I began my journey at Elder Henry Newby's church, the United Church of God. He preached the sermon that sent me on this path. The title of the sermon was "Count the Cost"—and he preached that sermon twice a year, every year. In my Bible, I would mark down notes about what was preached and taught each Sunday. Over several years, I began to see a pattern. At the same time every year, he would preach that same sermon: "Count the Cost."

In that sermon, I learned that there was a cost to pay. Old folks used to say salvation is free, but it will cost you everything. It costs to step out into nothing. It costs to venture where you have never been before. It costs to follow the voice of God wherever the quiet, still small voice of God leads you. It is going to cost you something.

That sermon was a milestone in my life. I remember it, and I cherish it to this day. Anyone beginning a new journey should count the cost. As the scripture asks, who goes to build a house without counting the cost? Indeed, who goes on a journey without counting the cost of what you will need to complete that journey? We need to be ready to let go of *everything*, whenever God calls us forth into a new revelation.

Go learn.

When I was ordained in the African Baptist Church, the Reverend David Hoover preached the charge. That sermon was called, "Go learn." That was another turning point in my life. He charged me always to continue to seek, always to continue my education, and to tell anyone that questioned me, "Go learn." He said, "Anybody who does not understand what it is to be gay or lesbian or bisexual or transgender, tell them, 'Go learn.'" He said, "Anybody who questions your religious practice, whether it is about baptism or speaking in tongues or anything else, tell them, 'Go learn.'"

I have kept that phrase close in my treasure chest of tools and resources for my journey. From that time forth, I counted the cost, and I went and studied. I learned more and more through the years—on my own, in college, in seminary. I continue to learn from books and classes and conversations. When anybody asks me anything, to this day, I encourage them to go learn for themselves.

You see, I can't teach anyone and I can't do anything for you. I can only point you in a direction. I can give you some books, some ideas, some suggestions, and some authors—but you have to go learn for yourself. I cannot cause a person to learn. Remember, everybody learns at their own pace. So, I took the Reverend Hoover's charge to heart. Go learn.

Undressing Jesus

The third important turning point—the one that took me "off the deep end"—was a sermon by Bishop Yvette Flunder. She called it "Undressing Jesus." For the past 15 years or so, I have been undressing and disrobing my Jesus until he was naked and unashamed.

Bishop's sermon addressed all of the dogma that has risen around all of the various traditions. We have surrounded Jesus with superficiality and tried to place Jesus in a box. From the big hats and the fancy robes to the smells and the bells, we have put everything from nice shoes to formal church protocols ahead of being the Body of Christ, filled with Love for our neighbor.

Each generation in Christianity added another layer of what they thought Jesus looked like, sounded like, and prioritized in his lifetime. Undressing Jesus means taking off those layers—taking off the fancy clothes, dropping the academic theology, and removing all of the pretense. I got back to the basics of what Jesus taught and showed us with his life—so much so that many of my church friends could no longer recognize him.

Age of Aquarius

Even today, God is still coming, again and again, in different people all over the world. Sometimes, Christians get closed off. We think that because the Christian Bible stopped at the Book of Revelation that there is no more sacred text—and no more revelations to be had.

However, as I explored beyond Christianity, I found other incarnations of my Jesus. I have kept my naked Jesus, dragging him everywhere I go—and everywhere I go, I always find Jesus! Because Jesus was not just a man. Jesus is an incarnation of God Almighty.

However, people are beginning to wake up in this Age of Aquarius. We are realizing that the story is not done being written. There are other books being written even now. There are new revelations being revealed. God is still speaking.

The Age of Aquarius is an age of knowledge, an age of awakening, and an age of awareness. More and more, people are waking up. You hear it all the time, "Wake up!" or "Come awake!" or "Stay woke!" It is time for us to get it together. That is my hope—that we begin to get together. It has to start with each of us as individuals. You have to get to know it for yourself before you can begin to share it with someone else. You have to get to a place where you know that you know, so that you will be ready when they challenge you.

There are people who will think you have lost your way. There will be people who will try to get you back on *their* straight and narrow—back into the limits of their old traditions and practices. Religious folk keep calling for peace, but we have not had peace! Ever! They will try to draw you back into the same ways that already have not been working. We need to count the cost and be ready for that.

You will never have peace, until you realize that you *are* Peace and that your neighbor is Peace, *also*; until you realize that you are Love *and* that your neighbor is Love, also. Stop looking at it any other way than that!

For the past 40 years, I have been seeking and searching. My journey took me from Christianity to Judaism and into the Eastern traditions like Buddhism and Hinduism. In this process, I found my own path. I am no longer an adherent of anyone else's religion. I am a theistic atheist. I am a believing non-believer. I found the right road for me. I created and customized my own religion to meet my spiritual needs and to help me grow into the person that I am becoming.

This journey has freed me. I came to understand the Truth—the Truth that the only thing there is *is* God. Now, don't get me wrong. There are plenty of things that are real enough in this world, but they still are not Truth. I can admit to the reality of sickness, disease, poverty, and oppression, but I have learned to allow the Truth to shine through even in the midst of those things. That allows me to live this victory—this peaceful, wholesome, happy life of freedom. That is what my journey has been about.

I will always continue to seek out fellowship with other believers, regardless of what religion, faith, or denomination they do (or do not) follow. I enjoy being in the company of believers because we are all one. If you are planted in a particular church, shul, synagogue, or temple, then be rooted there. I do not *want* to uproot your life! I only ask that you keep growing. Go learn.

I am very happy with my journey. I want to work with others to bring heaven to earth, to let other people know that as it is in heaven, so it is on earth. I believe that begins with being freed from the illusions that separate us really to appreciate our oneness.

In Peace,

The Reverend Jonathon Thunderword
Dallas, Texas
April 2020

Acknowledgments

To every spiritual sibling who has ever encouraged me to put myself on paper, thank you for believing in me and helping me to imagine that this could be possible.

To Bishop Yvette Flunder, thank you for supporting me endlessly through my development, transitions, and many wanderings.

To the Rev. Dr. Dorsey O. Blake, thank you for being my mentor at the Church for the Fellowship for All Peoples in San Francisco, California. I also honor the Rev. Dr. Howard Thurman as my ancestor in understanding the mysteries of the universe. I am grateful for his leadership through his writings and the church he co-founded.

To the Rev. Monica Joy Cross, thank you for so many intellectual and theological conversations through the years, which have informed this book.

To Koach Baruch Frazier, thank you for critical feedback on a draft of the text. To Nancy Krody, thank you for copy-editing advice.

To my editor and publisher, Mx Chris Paige, thank you for having the courage to take a chance on me. Thank you for keeping after me to move ahead with this project and for working diligently behind the scenes to make it possible. It has been a blessing to work so closely and creatively with you.

To my wife, Triptta Cohen-Thunderword, thank you for supporting me and encouraging me in every way possible. This book would not have been possible without your support as sound technician, secretary, coach, and proofreader. I love you.

To the Universe for being my everything.

Introduction

As my ancestors are free from slavery,
I am free from the slavery of religion.

Thelma "Butterfly" McQueen quoted in the
Atlanta Journal and Constitution on October 8, 1989

A picture is worth a thousand words. This picture speaks volumes: An enslaved Black man escaped to an encampment of the Union Army near Baton Rouge, Louisiana, in April 1863 (during the U.S. Civil War). This photograph was taken during the medical examination as Peter enlisted to serve in the Army. No surname was collected.

The photograph was widely circulated through the North by anti-slavery advocates, though we do not know what became of Peter after the photo was taken. When published in *Harper's Weekly*, the photo reached a massive audience but listed the man's name as "Gordon" (for no apparent reason). His image was used for abolitionist fundraising, accompanied by notes clarifying that he had done nothing to "deserve" such treatment. It was quite a spectacle.

In the picture, raised welts disfigure Peter's back. Northerners were surprised and appalled at the sight of this constellation of scars, but Southerners and enslaved African-Americans were all too familiar with the

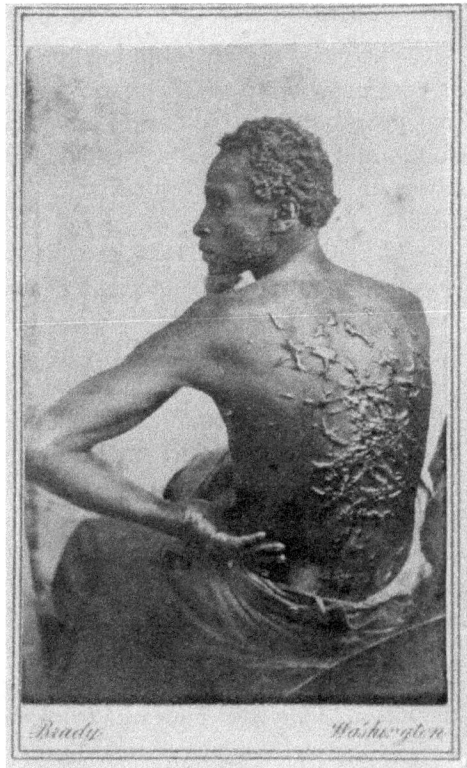

kinds of abuse that might leave such enduring marks.

The welts left by religion are typically less visible, but no less enduring. Each strike against one's very soul is an experience that leaves its mark on the individual. My flesh has born many such marks, brutally placed and without mercy, by those who would say they were only trying to help me. My well-being was scourged again and again: lashes to my self-esteem; assaults on the beauty of my spirit; violations of my body, as well as my soul—always with the expectation that I would submit, endlessly to such corrections.

One bad religious experience would have been sufficient, but I have been struck again and again. Each one of the many religious traditions that I have followed or visited throughout my journey from Christianity toward freedom is its own story and relationship. In this book, I will provide highlights from many different encounters that have left a mark on me.

Bruises do heal with time. Even after scars become less tender, they stick around to tell their story and help us to remember. I became disfigured, but I survived, and I am claiming my story. I know that I am not alone—and I believe that we would all benefit from having more space to share our stories. I believe that we have more in common than we might think.

With this book, I want to share my testimony of freedom. However, in order for you to understand my journey, I need to show you some of the scars that I carry. In most settings, I learn not to talk about these stories. While I may run my fingers over my own scars privately sometimes, we are typically encouraged to cover such wounds up for the sake of others. Most people are uncomfortable hearing much about struggle, even when it does not challenge their religious sensibilities. In such a world, it is no small task to take off my shirt to let others examine the lines on my back.

All this to say: Writing this book and reviewing my past have been uncomfortable for me—and it may be uncomfortable for you to read. I have had to take breaks, set limits, find support, and tend to my own needs. I encourage you to do likewise. Please be gentle with yourself.

Now that I am free, I sing along with my sister, Thelma "Butterfly" McQueen, "I am free! I am free from the slavery of religion."

I started out just trying to get away from Christianity, but, as I moved away, I also got free from organized religion more generally. I have carried not only a bruised and battered body with me but also trophies and souvenirs from my battles—proof of what I have been through: Krishna statue and crosses and candles and incense and different articles of clothing and even different scriptures that have endeared themselves to my heart. I will be sharing some of these souvenirs with you as well.

When someone gets shot, the surgeon will pull out the bullet, but the patient may decide to keep that bullet to remind them what they have endured. These traditions have wounded me, but they have also sustained me. I carry many reminders of how far I have come. You may see me at a religious ritual wearing *kippah* or *kufi* or *tzitzit* or even a clergy collar. These souvenirs remind me where I have come from. And, as they say, if you don't remember where you come from, you might go back to repeat things. I certainly do not want to go backwards.

There are hundreds of websites, books, and even organizations to support LGBT+ folk in healing from and reconciling with all kinds of religious traditions. There is space to acknowledge those struggles in community but usually only if your goal is to pick up that religious mantle again in some way. Unfortunately, there is typically little space for agnostics, skeptics, humanists, atheists, and other free thinkers. We need the balm of community, too.

Regardless of how we identify religiously or philosophically, many of us have suffered from post traumatic stress symptoms, religious trauma, and other kinds of abuse in religious settings. My program, Finding Another Right Road Authentically and Holistically (FARRAH) is designed to assist with unpacking such challenges and setting a new course that truly suits your needs. I will talk more about that in the Afterword.

I am no guru. I certainly do not have all the answers. I am still very much on the journey myself. So, my story is intended only to be an example—more "possibility model" than role model. With that in mind, each section of my story ends with one or more questions to help you look at your own experiences and needs. I encourage you to take notes (there is extra space at the back of this book) about where you agree or disagree with me as well as where you have had similar or different experiences. These are the building blocks that you can use to build your own shelter from the storm.

So, let us begin at my beginning . . .

Chapter 1

Beginning with Christianity

Over the last 50 years, I have run into many types of Christianity. All of them claim to be the *true* Christianity. Each one claims to be the only way to live a holy life acceptable unto the Lord, the only one that's going to get you to heaven, and the only one to cleanse your sins. Each one claims that if you submit yourself to their particular Christian teaching, you will be righteous and right in the eyes of God.

Now, I understand that there is actually no such thing as a "right" Christianity. In fact, there are many varieties of Christianity. Each has its own traditions and rules, perks and quirks about them, but they all claim to be Christianity. I want to start this story of "Christendom to Freedom" by telling you about a few of the kinds of Christianity that I have explored.

Episode 1—Beginnings

The first kind of Christianity that I was involved with was pretty typical. I was born and raised in a Christian family, and I grew up in a Christian church. I was taught to believe in the Lord Jesus Christ. I was taught that if you don't sin, if you "do good" and obey the rules, if you follow their Bible and do what they say, then you can be saved.

That teaching included the death, burial, and resurrection of Jesus Christ. It taught that Jesus is my Lord and Savior who came to save me from hell—and from my wretched life. That was my first taste of Christianity as a kid—and my first introduction to Jesus. It was pretty basic—an A-B-C elementary kind of Christianity.

Yet, this basic Christianity was also a fear-based, "God sitting in heaven" kind of approach. In other words, their God was a white man with a white beard sitting on a white throne, looking down at us in judgment. That was my introduction to Christianity. God and Jesus were both definitely white men, and I was taught to honor and respect them. That kind of respect gave me a great love for Caucasian people, and, in the long run, it also would teach me that I can never be like God or Jesus. After all, he was white, and I always have been and always will be Black.

Meanwhile, everywhere I looked in this Christian community, I saw a lot of hatred. I did not see compassion or forgiveness. In fact, I saw no moral fiber whatsoever. The minister and the deacons were always on the "down low," doing something—whether that was gambling, adultery, or something else. They really didn't teach a lot of acceptance of anybody, except the Christians in their particular denomination. In fact, you really had to be in their particular local church to matter to them in any real way. It was a very narrow and judgmental way of being in the world

Your Story

Most of us who grow up in the United States learned something about Christianity through our childhood, regardless of what our family of origin did or didn't practice. What were your first impressions of Christianity?

Episode 2—Commitment

The hypocrisy of the Christianity of my childhood did not suit me. However, I stayed for many years because that is where I was born and raised. I did not know any other way. By the age of 26, I had had enough, and I could not take it anymore. I knew that the God I loved and the Jesus that I understood simply were not present in the ways they were representing Christianity at all.

I began my first search for a more authentic Christianity—a Christianity that I could practice and a Christianity that could help me to grow. I landed in a very fundamentalist, but loving congregation, called the United Church of God. They seemed familiar in many ways—similar to the church of my upbringing. Everybody was family. Everybody loved and celebrated each other. What is mine is yours. What is yours is mine. We were caring and praying and loving one another and trying to do the right thing.

In this community, I also learned to knock on doors with a religious tract in my hand. We were regularly out in the streets and parking lots, handing out tracts, brochures, and flyers. We were trying to win souls, because Jesus is coming—and he is coming soon! At the end of each gathering at the church, they would say, "See you here, there, or in the air"—which meant they would see you back here at the church, or they would meet you in heaven (if and when the rapture came). "Getting to heaven" was their entire focus.

This same church also taught me some helpful things. They were extremely focused on the Bible. They taught that in order to know the Word, you had to know the Word. So, the first thing they gave to any new member was a *Scofield Reference Bible*. Every member of the church had one, along with a concordance and a commentary. These were their three main Bible reference tools. We might also use a dictionary or a map or other resource material, but it was drilled into us that we should not come to a worship service or a class without our *Scofield Bible*, the concordance, and the commentary in hand. So, in this version of Christianity, I really begin to study the Bible in-depth.

I was presenting as a woman at the time. I really wasn't allowed to do much of anything. I could not be a minister. I could not preach. I could not even get in the pulpit to make an announcement.

Living as a lesbian was out of the question because of my strong conviction and the teaching I was under. I did not want to "go to hell" over that! In fact, it was this particular brand of religion that had me seeking out a local ex-gay conversion ministry. I learned about Exodus International, and my pastor wrote a letter of recommendation for me. There was an Exodus center nearby where they tried to brainwash me. It was actually a horrible thing, but I will spare you those details.

Women were expected to be totally submissive. Since I was already married and divorced, I would never ever be allowed to marry again in that tradition as long as my first husband was still alive. They believed that once you were married, you were always married. So, if you did anything else with anybody, you were committing adultery. I was so committed to this way of thinking that I tried to remarry the man that I had previously divorced, because I did not want to live in sin! That said, I divorced him for good reason the first time! So, the second try did not last more than a minute or so.

The church taught that you could have "homosexual" feelings as long as you did not follow through with any physical acts. Of course, once you acted on those feelings, you would be "on your way to hell." I lived with a woman for some time. We were both in the church and had similar "inclinations," but we were entirely committed to the church's teachings. We had even been re-baptized as a sign of our repentance from our past sins.

We both worked hard to comply with their teachings, but, ultimately, they still did not trust me. After all of the pain and fasting and praying that we went through, they still put me out of the church. They went from "just don't act on your feelings" to making assumptions about my relationship with this female housemate. Suddenly, I was out and on my own again. It was brutal.

Your Story

What do you know about the Christian Bible? Have you studied it first hand? Or have you only heard about it from others?

Episode 3—Openly Gay

I am grateful that the Metropolitan Community Church (MCC) caught me when I fell out from fundamentalism. Troy Perry will always be in my heart for the gift that he has offered so many. I read his first book, *The Lord Is My Shepherd—and, He Knows I'm Gay* (1987). That was a long time ago, but it remains a good read for those who may be coming out of anti-gay, fundamentalist Christianity. It provided me with the encouragement that I needed—that the Lord was still shepherding me, that God was with me and loving me, even if I was gay.

It was through MCC that I first began to imagine that there could be a Christianity that might accept me as a "gay" person. I had, literally, never heard of that before. I studied the Bible again through MCC and learned new ways of reading it. I learned about a Christian tradition that is affirming and full of hope. Remember, the world was a different place in the 1980s and even the 1990s. There was no general-purpose internet. We could not imagine social media—and the language of "transgender" hadn't been invented yet (at least not in the way that we use it today).

I went to MCC's Samaritan College, where I learned about human sexuality and the church. This was a totally different way of doing church! We talked about oral sex and anal sex and vaginal sex and everything else. They considered that to be important knowledge for ministers of the Gospel to have. I continued to grow in both spiritual knowledge and practical wisdom.

While I still have friends in the MCC to this day, it was not the perfect church for me. I definitely value the landing place they offered me on my journey. However, as I healed, I felt called to serve all of the marginalized on the street, such as sex workers, transgender women, and those experiencing homelessness. I wanted to reach out to those who were mentally and emotionally and physically challenged. God had laid this kind of ministry on my heart—to heal the wounded and bind up the brokenhearted.

However, the particular MCC church where I was participating did not support that kind of "whosoever" outreach. They did not want a bunch of alcoholics, drug addicts, and homeless people participating. They did not want that "element" in the church. They would hold a food drive or offer a Thanksgiving meal to those who were struggling, but really they only wanted to support folk who were same-gender-loving. They might engage with a drag queen as part of a fundraiser, as entertainment, but transgender identity was not even a real part of the conversation at that time.

I was pressing for us to share with others, who were also God's children—and a part of this challenge was quietly about race. The

4

congregation was mostly white and so they simply did not face the kind of discrimination that African-American lesbian, gay, bisexual, and transgender people were experiencing. In other words, people who looked like them were much less likely to experience homelessness, participate in survival economies, or otherwise drown their despair in drugs or alcohol. The "whosoever" crowd, "those" people, that "element"—they were all very likely to be people of color, specifically African-American, even though they were not explicitly talking about race.

Meanwhile, I wanted to be inclusive of everybody. I wanted us to be reaching out into every nook and cranny to all kinds of folk who were in need, regardless of whatever! However, that went over like a lead balloon and brought me into conflict with others in the church. So, I left MCC.

Your Story

What values are most important to you? Have those values been reflected in (faith) communities you have been involved in?

Episode 4—Small Groups

After MCC, I found the Victory Life World Outreach Center. This was a group that was focused on evangelism, developing spiritual authority, and teaching demonology. You had to learn to recognize demons, to cast out demons, and to engage in spiritual warfare.

Not only would we learn scripture, we would sing scripture. We literally surrounded ourselves with the Word. I was immersed in religious activity, not just in terms of what I believed in my head, but in terms of how I was living my life, from moment to moment in every way.

It was a huge church, but your cell groups were never more than about 25 people. This was like another big family, and the smaller groups were very close-knit. If any small group got too big, they would break it up into smaller groups. This was also part of their growth strategy overall. There was a commitment to evangelism, and their outreach resonated with me. It seemed like it offered a practical kind of engagement with the world that would really make a difference for everyone involved.

So, I got involved in a small group. At that time, I was married to a female impersonator (also referred to as a drag queen). When s/he went to worship with me, s/he would dress in six inch heels. Of course, it was a sign of care and respect that she was getting dressed up, but after that first time s/he came to the altar with me, they started investigating my life a bit more. You can imagine how that went! So, off I went on my merry way again, to look for another Christianity that might be a better fit.

Your Story

Are you more comfortable in larger groups or in smaller groups? How much do you seek out spiritual community?

Episode 5—Radically Inclusive

Next, I came across a radically inclusive Christianity where everybody was included. They were serving the homeless, and they were serving people living with AIDS. They had folk who were struggling with drug addiction, and they had folk who were sick and afflicted and marginalized in all kinds of ways. I was down with the City of Refuge UCC really quick! These were my people!

I was finally with church folk who understood what I was saying about reaching out to the least of these, the marginalized, and everyone who is hurting. Their approach to scripture emphasized those who were living on the margins: the poor, the sick, the homeless, and the outcast. They wanted to make space at the table for everyone who was downtrodden, including but not limited to same-gender-loving and transgender folk. They understood Jesus to be someone who was about empowerment. They understood Jesus to be someone who was living right there on the margins *with* us.

By that point, I had been out there on the battlefield since 1981. I had been working with people with HIV and AIDS. I had been working with addicts. I had been working with people in survival economies (for instance, selling drugs or sex work). I had been working with same-gender-loving people, drag queens, and transgender people. Finally, I had found a church home where I could bring somebody who was infected, who was sick, or who was in need. It was wonderful to finally find my people.

Your Story

Do you expect religion to focus on belief or practice? How does belief and practice connect in your life? Is it easier to compromise on one or the other?

Chapter 2

Converting to Judaism

I loved (and still love) City of Refuge UCC, but I remained full of questions. I had always been a seeker, and I was still seeking greater wisdom. I remember my Bishop Flunder's telling me, "Hey, you got to go and build bridges and connect people." So she gave me permission and encouragement to explore.

Before I could tell anybody else about Finding Another Right Road Authentically and Holistically, I had to find it for myself. So, I kept searching. I sure did love me some Jesus, but I could never fully reconcile the Christian message with my understanding of Jesus. Even after I found my people, Christianity was not working for me entirely. Eventually, I found Judaism—the Judaism of Jesus.

Episode 1—Falling in Love

I first walked into Congregation Sha'ar Zahav in San Francisco, California, in November 2007. I went there to sing with the Transcendence Gospel Choir. Transcendence was a transgender choir organized out of City of Refuge UCC. We had been invited to perform at a transgender memorial service. That in itself was an exciting opportunity because we had to make a careful decision about what song a (Christian) Gospel choir was going to sing in a Jewish *shul*. We decided to sing, "I Need You to Survive" (and one other selection).

We went and sang the songs, and then much of the choir left because they had other things to do that day. I decided to stay for the entire service. It was during that service that everything changed—when I saw that beautiful Torah scroll unrolled before my eyes. They keep the Torah in a big beautiful ark. When they open up the ark, the Torah has the most beautiful covering with handles on it. Even the handles have covers on them! The cover for the Torah is always made out of silver. They have a velvet cover over that.

You are never allowed to touch the Torah with your hands—ever. So, as they brought out the Torah and unrolled it and took off all the coverings, there was a yad. The yad is a little pointer that you touch the Torah with while you are reading. You use the yad to help you to keep your place (without touching it). The entire affair was an elaborate display of care for this sacred scroll.

I remember that what really caught my eye was that beautiful sparkling brass plate over the top. The Torah was so beautiful that I could not take my eyes off it. It was different from any of the many Bibles that I had ever read. I said to myself, "I want to know what is in this book!"

So, I stayed that Saturday, but then I also continued to come back to *shul* after that. I would go to *shul* on Fridays and Saturdays—and I was also attending City of Refuge UCC on Sundays. After attending on a regular basis for a while, I knew that I wanted to convert to Judaism.

Your Story

Have you ever been doing one thing and found yourself drawn into something else unexpectedly?

Episode 2—Conversion

It is a Jewish tradition that when a person asks to convert, they always decline your request at first. They want you to be really, really sure about making this decision and all that it entails. So, the first time I asked, they said, "No."

I continued to go to Torah study on Saturday mornings and attended all the services and all the programs that they offered. I got really involved in the community. The next time I asked, the rabbi said "Yes." So, I was allowed to take classes related to conversion.

Rabbi Reuben Zellman, who is also a trangender man, was my mentor during that process. He walked me through an entire year of learning and preparation for my conversion. I explored all of Judaism, not just the Torah. I also learned about the history, all the holidays, the traditions, and more. There was a lot of reading and I learned a lot.

I completed my conversion process in 2009, about 18 months after I started attending *shul*. At that point, I took on a Jewish name: Yonah Yehudah son of Abraham and Sarah. I took "*Yonah*" in honor of the prophet Jonah who I was already familiar with from my experiences in Christian tradition. Jonah means "dove" and it also means "bear." Doves are gentle and bears are the totally opposite. So, it suited me quite well as a both/and kind of person. I chose "*Yehudah*" because Jesus was from the tribe and line of Judah. That connection to my roots in Christianity still felt important to me.

After you choose a name, you go through a ritual purification bath. While I had been baptized several times in Christianity, this was going to be

8

different. When you go to the *mikvah*, you first undress and take a really thorough shower. I had to scrub carefully from my bottom to my top. I had to remove all of my jewelry, even my wedding band. Everything came off until every stitch of anything was gone except "me, myself, and I." I was clean as a whistle!

When you get submerged into the water of the *mikveh*, you go all the way to the bottom. At the bottom of the bath, you get into the fetal position like when you were in your mother's womb. For me, it felt similar to a Christian baptism. Arguably, Christian baptism evolved from the *mikveh* cleansing required of all Jewish converts. The *mikveh* can represent the mother's womb and this is a rebirth.

Then, you rise up and you come up to the top of the water. You repeat that process three times—three times into the water and the fetal position and also three times coming up. Because you are completely naked, this is a more private ceremony than most Christian baptisms. However, someone does accompany you to verify that you completed the process properly. My witness was a young, African-American, transgender man who was also a part of the *shul*.

Adult circumcision is not as severe as it is for babies. Because I am a transgender man (not a cisgender man), I did not have to be circumcised at all. However, I am a stickler for details and I wanted to be able to say that I had observed all of the Jewish law. Because I was entering into a blood covenant, I felt that it would not be a blood covenant without blood. So, I wanted to be circumcised. This involved a prick to my penis—enough to draw out some blood into a small sponge. This blood was given as a part of my commitment to being a Jew and joining in covenant with *HaShem*.

To be frank, as a Black, transgender Jew, I wanted to be prepared if someone ever challenged me. Well, did you go to the *mikveh*? Were you circumcised? I completed the entire process and all of the requirements of becoming a Jew. I got a certificate saying that I had been circumcised according to Jewish law.

You Story

Are there any parts of your life where you feel pressure to somehow prove yourself authentic?

Episode 3—Commitment

I got to read the Torah portion for the week that I was coming into covenant. The Torah portion for that week was from the Book of Exodus. It talked about how God brings God's people out of bondage with a mighty hand (Exodus 13:3). This meant a lot to me because I thought to myself that I was being brought up out of Christianity by Jesus into the Jewish faith. Jesus was my Moses, bringing me up out of slavery. I had to speak from that text for 10 to 15 minutes.

This was a very touching moment for me. After I had been through all these requirements for conversion, here I was, back in the synagogue up close as they got the Torah out once again. The rabbi held the Torah as he proclaimed that I would be yoked with the Jewish people and also with the Torah itself. From that moment, I have had all the rights, privileges, and concerns of everything that comes with being Jewish. I have been a Jew from that day forward—forever.

You can never "un-Jew" yourself. I will always be a Jew and always will be recognized as a Jew, no matter what happens. I am in it, and, according to Jewish law, no one is supposed to ask me if I converted or if I was born a Jew. That is because there is no difference. When you are a Jew—especially if you have observed all of the requirements to become a Jew—you are a Jew. Period. That's it.

So the rabbi placed the Torah on my shoulder, because I had taken on this burden and this yoke and this commitment. I was taking a step always to be a part of the community, always to honor the community, always to honor the Torah, and always to obey the Torah law. It was very meaningful to me to be able to take up the Torah in that way as I formally entered into Judaism.

Your Story

What does commitment mean to you? Has your spiritual journey involved formal steps to embody or demonstrate your commitments?

Episode 4—Studying the Law

Once I converted, my Jewish journey was not done! I continued to study Torah. I was impressed by how much depth there is in Judaism. The Torah is the first five books of both the Christian and Hebrew Bible— Genesis, Exodus, Leviticus, Deuteronomy, and Numbers. It is also called the Pentateuch (meaning "five scrolls") or the law of Moses. This Torah is the foundation of the Jewish faith.

There are Jews who have never seen other Jewish texts like the *Mishna* or the *Talmud*. They only have the Torah. For a long, long time, Ethiopian Jews and Chinese Jews and Jews in other parts of the world did not have any books except for the Torah. However, because they observed all of Torah law, they were still considered Jewish.

Observing the Torah is the baseline for being a Jew. It is everything to the Jewish people, so, there is a lot of focus on the Torah. In some synagogues, they do not teach anything but Torah. They do not teach the writings of the prophets. They do not teach poetry or history. They focus on the law and only the law, all the time. However, in other synagogues, there may be a portion from the book of the prophet Jeremiah or from the Psalms or from some other Jewish text. Yet, it is still the Torah that is held in the highest esteem.

When I began to read the Torah, I really had to adjust. Of course, these were scriptures that I have been reading all my life as a Christian. However, now I was reading these texts through Jewish eyes and Jewish history and Jewish understanding. I learned the Hebrew language, too. So, now I was understanding more details about how the language shaped the meaning of the text. It was the same document, but it was entirely different from what I had previously been taught about the Hebrew scripture in all those Christian churches!

Beyond the Torah, we have the *Mishna* and *Talmud*, that are commentaries on the Torah that have been passed down through the centuries. These books are broken down into sections, so we can study it bit by bit. There are also certain texts associated with particular sects of Judaism—and each of these texts was entirely new to me. Many Jews study the works of Maimonides. The *Tanya* is a prominent Hasidic book of wisdom. The *Zohar* is an important text in Kabbalah, which details the mysteries of Creation. In fact, this mystical tradition is considered so powerful (and potentially dangerous) that you have to study Torah for many years before you will even be allowed to begin studying the Kabbalah

When I began my conversion, I had to choose a subject to study during that year of preparation. I chose to study the Sabbath. There were pages and pages and books and books on the Sabbath: how to observe the Sabbath, what to do during the *Shabbat* service, the code of ethics around Sabbath observance. I really wanted to study the ethics around Jewish law in general, but I could not do all of that in just one year! So, I focused my attention on the Sabbath.

I always wanted to know why Christians did what they did. In Sunday school at church, they said, "Thou shalt not steal," and "Thou shalt not lie," and all the rest of the commandments. Christians spent a lot of time on the "thou shall *not*," but they did not give me much on the "thou *shall*." So, I really appreciated the details of Jewish teaching where they break down every commandment in excruciating detail—not just the Ten Commandments handed down at Sinai, but all 613 commandments in the Torah!

When you study, you get every detail down to whether or not you can break a twig on the Sabbath or how many cubits you can walk on the Sabbath. I like how organized it is. Everything is very orderly, so you can observe the law faithfully. They work to make it plain and simple so everyone knows what is expected. That meant that I knew exactly what I had to do. I appreciated that.

HaShem is what Jews call God. It means "the name," because God's actual name is too sacred to be spoken. When *HaShem* asked the Hebrew people if they would become the chosen people, they answered by saying, "We will do what you say." They were willing to do what God had asked them before they even knew what God was going to ask them!

Now, most people will want to know more details upfront about what will be required. What does the law consist of? What will we have to do? The Jewish people said, "We will do whatever it is you say that we should do." All of the laws and interpretations of the law came about after they had already made that decision.

For me, that is an important part of being in relationship with God. I want to be obedient to God regardless of what comes along the way. To me, that is real faith. That is the kind of faith the Jewish people showed when they entered into this new covenant, this new kind of relationship with God.

Your Story

Do you find clearly stated rules helpful? Or challenging? Do you expect full disclosure before making a commitment?

Episode 5—Tradition(s)

I followed Jesus into Judaism in part because I wanted to know what Jesus did as a Jew. Becoming a Jew made things much more clear to me, even just from reading about the ancient customs. For instance, in the story of the woman who touched the hem of Jesus' garment (Luke 8:40–48), I always imagined that she was simply on her knees and reached to touch the hem of his garment. But, in Judaism, I learned about *tzitzit* at the edge of an observant Jew's robe. *Tzitzit* are these four tassels that hang from your garment as commanded in Torah.

The first time I read about *tzitzit*, I realized that Jesus must have worn *tzitzit*, too. At that time, I had not yet converted to Judaism, but I wanted to follow Jesus. So, I also started to wear *tzitzit*. According to everything I have ever read, Jesus obeyed all the Jewish laws. They say he never broke one single law. So, Jesus must have been doing all of these things in order to be called "rabbi" and in order to have Jewish disciples following him.

Coming from a Christian background, I would connect everything I learned as a Jew to what I had learned before as a Christian. There is a Jewish prayer for when I put on the *tzitzit*. When I say this prayer, I visualize putting on the whole armor of God (Ephesians 6), so that I might be able to withstand trial and temptation. To me, the *tzitzit* is the whole armor of God. It is also a way for me to feel close to Jesus.

The *tzitzit* is a constant reminder. When I see them hanging down, I remember not to steal or commit other sins. The *tzitzit* remind me to walk in the right path all of the time. I still wear my *tzitzit* because I appreciate that reminder. When people see the *tzitzit*, they know that I am walking in covenant with God and that I obey the commandments of God.

Jews also have *tefillin*, which is a little black box that is worn on your head. Inside the black box are four hand-written Torah verses, such as the scripture about loving the Lord your God with all your heart (Deuteronomy 6:5). The head tefillin goes in the middle of my forehead and is attached with a strap. The head tefillin reminds me to always keep God's Word in my mind and that God is the head of my life. The head-tefillin is put on as a part of a morning prayer service.

There is also an arm-tefillin that gets wrapped around my arm. The arm-tefillin helps me remember the binding of Isaac (Genesis 22). For me, it also helps me remember that I am bound to Jesus. One of the straps goes around my finger like a ring. It represents that I am married to God. The other strap goes all the way up my arm to afix another black box with a scripture inside.

So, during morning prayer, I am expressing my commitment, literally, by binding myself to God and God's commandments. It also reminds me of the Christian scripture (Matthew 18:18) that anything bound on earth is also bound in heaven (and anything loosed on earth is also loosed in heaven). Every time I lay *tefillin*, I am reconnecting with the Divine. These traditions also help me to feel close to Jesus. Each time I take these physical actions, I am reminded of the connection that I have with Jesus and that God is the head of my life.

I have a prayer shawl—which is also a Jewish tradition. I cover my head and my face with the shawl. So, when I pray, it is like going into the tent of Abraham. As a Christian, I would say I was going into the prayer closet and closing the door behind me. In each case, when I close my eyes under the tent (or in the closet), it is just me and God. For me, that is such a quiet and a peaceful feeling to know that I am under God's care with his banner over me in love.

Your Story

Have you found any physical rituals or practices that help guide you and focus your attention on what is most important to you?

Chapter 3

Exploring Islam

My experience with Islam has been an "on again and off again" experience. I was attracted to it back in the early days when the Nation of Islam was at its peak strength. We, as Black people, were trying to find ourselves. As Malcolm X said, we had been hoodwinked and bamboozled—and we were looking for some answers because the Christianity of the slave masters had not always been truthful with us.

Episode 1—Black Pride

Malcolm was a powerful minister for the Honorable Elijah Muhammad in the Nation of Islam. He had tremendous passion. I would listen to him back in those days, and I was like, "Wow! This man is really saying something!" Still, Martin Luther King, Jr., had his dream and he was also moving forward. In the secular world, the Black Panthers were inspiring, and we also had folk like James Brown singing, "Say it loud, I'm Black and I'm proud."

There was a lot going on at that time! As African-Americans (though that identity language came later), we wanted to find out who we were as a people. The Nation of Islam was bringing a sense of unity and Black pride. They also had an understanding of our original religion—which they said was Islam. So, Islam became part of my early exploration. It stood apart as tradition where my Blackness was actually valued—and not some kind of an afterthought.

Your Story

Are there prophets, religious or not, who have inspired you to embrace all of who you are?

Episode 2—Prophets

Unfortunately, that egg broke, as it were. It broke first for Malcolm—when he realized that some of the teachings of the Honorable

Elijah Muhammad were not true. Malcolm saw that some of Elijah Muhammad's conduct was not as ethical as one might have expected. As a result, Malcolm left the Nation of Islam and went to discover for himself how Muslims in other parts of the world treat each other.

To me, there is nothing worse than being in an organization where the leaders that I hold in high esteem betray my trust. It is easy to forget that each and every person who speaks for God is still human. I think that this experience with the Nation of Islam shaped my journey in some important ways that were not immediately obvious. I learned that we have to take responsibility for our own beliefs and our own conduct at every turn.

Your Story

Have you ever felt betrayed by a religious leader or another leader who you trusted? How did that impact your relationship with the tradition(s) that they represented?

Episode 3—Unity

Malcolm took a new name when he left the Nation of Islam. He became El-Hajj Malik El-Shabazz. Shabazz traveled the world and did a pilgrimage to Mecca—called the Hajj. He discovered that there were no Blacks or whites in Islam. While still made of imperfect humans, Muslim communities, even to this day, are religiously organized to challenge any tendency that places one kind of person over another. Unlike the segregation he experienced in the U.S., Shabazz walked alongside people of many races and nationalities during his pilgrimage.

Similarly, I appreciate the sense of unity in Muslim prayer. Everyone stands side by side, shoulder to shoulder, foot to foot—all kneeling at one time. No matter if you are a lawyer or a doctor or a garbage man, when we pray at mosque, everyone is equal. We bow as one people before one God. It is a beautiful sight to see, and I still enjoy going to mosque just to pray. There is a very special energy when we all line up together for prayer.

I also love praying five times a day. It is a wonderful reminder to check in, to breathe, to remember that you are not alone. I wear my hat—it is called *kufi* cap—to remember that *Allah* is the head of my life. Praying five times a day to *Allah* reminds me that God is the one who controls me and guides me at all times. It is a reminder to be respectful of the knowledge that God has put within me—to hold that wisdom within me close at all times.

Your Story

Are there teachings or traditions which have inspired you to find a common humanity among people of different backgrounds and experiences?

Episode 4—Separation

Despite that sense of unity overall, the separation between men and women in Islam was a problem for me. Much like Orthodox Jews, women and men usually pray separately in Islam. In Jewish tradition, the *mechitza* is the wall or petition that divides the men from the women. It can be a very challenging obstacle for transgender people. In Islam, the women may be in an entirely different room! Once I started studying the Qur'an, I also began to struggle with how violent some of the text is.

That said, I do believe that the Holy One sends different prophets to different people. Muhammed (Peace Be Upon Him) was the founder of the Muslim faith, which is closely connected to both Judaism and Christianity. Whether we say God or *Hashem* or *Allah*, we are talking about the same person—the Creator of the Universe! That Creator is the God of Abraham and Isaac and Jacob, the God of Jesus, and the God of Muhammad. These are all just different ways to speak about the same Divine Being working through different languages, cultures, and traditions.

Muhammad was certainly leading his people to be more loving and more kind. Indeed, some very beautiful things have come out of the religious tradition that he founded. Muhammad's teachings and intentions may get twisted here or there, but he did the best he could with the information he had. There will always be some people who try to turn a religion into a violent, hateful tradition, especially after the founder is gone. The same certainly could be said of Jesus and Christianity!

In any case, I had had enough trouble with gender issues in Christianity. I really did not need to add another layer of trauma around my gender. My transgender brothers in Islam would hide out and worry about being found out. So, Islam did not seem to be safe for or compatible with me as a Black transgender man. Where would I fit in? Why are men given more privilege? What about people who do not fit into these two categories of gender?

I was not ready to fight that battle, so it seemed best to leave. I packed all the goodness that I had gathered from Islam and took it with me, like packing a sandwich for lunch on a long journey. I am grateful for all the truth that was revealed to me through my experiences in Muslim community and tradition.

Your Story

Have you experienced religion primarily as a force that unites? Or primarily as a force that separates?

Chapter 4

More on Gender

I have lived my life in two realities. In one reality, I was perceived as a female, as a woman. In the other, I was perceived as a man living in a man's world. Sometimes, I was in two worlds at the exact same time—depending on who was looking at me. I had to get used to walking between the two worlds as I lived with both labels, trying to coexist. Learning to navigate two worlds has also been an important part of my journey toward freedom.

Episode 1—Deliverance

Being a lesbian in Christian tradition was a nightmare. Being a Christian and perceived as a female was difficult because it was commanded and demanded that I live the life of a "good Christian woman." As I grew older, that meant I was supposed to be a wife and have kids and teach Sunday school and sing in the choir and be obedient to a husband. I was to be submissive and stay in a "woman's place" (whatever that meant at the time)—and I really tried to live that out as best I could.

Even before we had language for "transgender," I had to deal with being treated poorly as a lesbian. When I was 11 years old, I was already grappling with being a lesbian and being a Christian. Being perceived as a lesbian involved all manner of negativity and scandal, but I wanted very much to live a good Christian lifestyle as a Black Baptist woman. So, I reached out to my Sunday school teacher and I told her that I love women and I felt like a man. I poured my little heart out to her, because I did not want to live in sin. I wanted to be delivered.

What did this adult woman do? She carried me into her bedroom and tried to molest me. I was only 11, but I was like, "No, no, no, no!" I knew that this was exactly what I was trying to get away from.

She said, "I am going to teach you what it is to be a lesbian in the Christian church and how you are going to survive." Her advice was, "We do the act. After it is completed, we both get down on our knees and we repent and ask God to forgive us." She said, "God will forgive us our sins because He is faithful and He will cleanse us from all unrighteousness."

She wanted us to keep going through that vicious cycle for the rest of our lives—and I suppose that *is* how *she* lived. Still, it was a lot to take in at the age of 11. My father raised me with integrity and a moral compass, so I knew that my Sunday school teacher's way was not the answer for me. I did not follow her advice at all.

I never went back to her house, but the struggle continued—and I could not seem to get away from the nightmare. At age 13, puberty was upon me and the temptation was growing even worse. Actually, *everything* was worse. So, this time, I went to my pastor. I went into his office, and I told him the same story of my struggle with this "demon."

The "good pastor" put me on his couch and he molested me, too. I remember his words clearly to this day: "I'm putting the Holy Ghost in you."

Now, I knew that was not right, either. So, I tried to tell people that the pastor had molested me. However, they saw him as a man of God who could do no wrong. Meanwhile, I was just a "sinful," "evil," "corrupt" lesbian and so they painted *me* as trying to cause trouble—to distract from my "terrible" ways.

At that point, I was over trying to grapple with my sexuality with these Baptist folks. Later, I grappled again with the Pentecostal folks, with fasting and prayer, but there was no release for me. Eventually, I knew it was time to go and find another way to cope because I had done everything I could possibly do to try and change.

Your Story

I am not alone in my experience with sexual abuse at the hands of religious leaders. Such experiences can have a lasting impact. Have you had any experiences that were anything like what I described?

Episode 2—Affirmation

When I started identifying as a transgender man, I was in a church that was very open and affirming of transgender people. This felt like a great opportunity to live my life to the fullest. They affirmed me. Until then, I was known as Joyce. Now, I was baptized with my new name, Jonathon. I was a deacon in the church. The name was changed on my membership certificate. This was all confirmed by the congregation, and it was wonderful!

I was a deacon in the church and I was ready to follow in the footsteps of my father and grandfather. It meant a lot to me to be appointed a deacon. My father and grandfather both had chaired the deacon boards in their respective churches. I always thought deacons had to be men, because they had always been men in all the churches I had ever attended up until then. There simply was no such thing as a female deacon in my early life. It was always a man's job, and no woman could ever have it. Even living as a lesbian in the church, it meant a lot for me to be a deacon. It meant even more for me to be able to follow in my father's footsteps as a male deacon.

Your Story

Have you ever struggled to find a place for some part of your story?

Episode 3—Toxic Masculinity

To this day, the word I hate most in the whole world is "bulldagger." In my hood, where I came from, a bulldagger was a cross-dresser—bulldaggers and butch dykes. This was a long time ago and a lot has changed since then. I really had to challenge what these words represented in order to bring healing to myself, but also to bring healing to those around me. It was like I was on this mission, especially once I started identifying as a man. I had to grapple with how the limited vocabulary we had then interacted with my understanding of what it meant to be a Christian man.

When people perceived me as a "bulldagger," they saw me not only as a woman who cross-dressed, but also as someone who was inappropriate with and dehumanizing to other women. That word meant that I was someone who was uncouth, touching, groping, and doing all manner of nonconsensual, disgusting things. This is part of why people stayed in the closet—to avoid such assumptions. It was why even gay churches had trouble accepting the butch dykes.

This was not so much about being a lesbian or a same-gender-loving person as it was about gender expression and social behavior more generally. We did not want to have "bulldaggers" in our church. This was not simply prejudice. It was more complicated than that. Some lesbians were dressing as men and acting as men—acting out all the negativity they had ever seen or heard of in men. They wanted to bring that toxic masculinity into the church.

It was a responsibility of a deacon like myself to try to redirect them and help them understand that there are different ways to be a man (or even just masculine) that do not involve treating women poorly. Remember, I really wanted to go out to evangelize the world. I wanted to let my fellow outcasts know that there was a place for us. So, I wanted to bring them into the fold.

However, there were also standards for how we needed to behave.

We could not abide blatantly abusive practices. Nobody was asking for "perfection." Still, most bulldaggers did not appreciate being told how to date or how much to drink or how to behave! They saw these parts of themselves as expressing a part of their freedom to be who they wanted to be.

Your Story

Does "freedom" mean no boundaries at all? What kind of values do you hold dear regardless of who someone is?

Episode 4—Sexism and Misogyny

Even inside open and affirming churches, it could be challenging to be living these two realities. Some churches were led by men and ended up being almost anti-female. The pastor, deacons, and officers were 99% male and they all seemed to buy into that "old boy" mentality. They had issues with women in leadership roles because they grew up in churches where women were not allowed to teach or do anything. They were breaking free from homophobia, but they still imagined church just the way they had grown up. They simply wanted gay men to be in charge—with no other changes.

On the other side of the coin, when females were in leadership and in the majority, men would have to take a step back. In those days, we had not even started to talk about non-binary gender identities. Men would be worried about being under the leadership of a woman because they were being made fun of by those who would say, "How can you be submitting to a woman?!"

Meanwhile, you might also have women congregants who were so attached to the idea of having male leadership that they were unwilling to respond to women who were in leadership. They, too, might say, "Nobody is going to take us seriously if women are in charge." Folk were same-gender-loving, but they were not *free*.

In these environments, there was not a lot of understanding about transgender men. I might be treated like a woman and expected to submit, if someone knew my birth history—or, I might be treated like a man and expected to stay over there with the good brothers, if they read me as male. However, I did not have the mentality of proving myself to be a "real man" with all of that ugliness, so fitting in as a different kind of man was still challenging. I had experience on both sides of this drama, so I knew what kind of harm was caused by treating people poorly.

We have grown a lot and learned a lot in the last few decades, but those were challenges that I faced even in open and affirming kinds of churches back in the day. Some of that sexism and misogyny still exists among liberal church folk today! Not everyone has done the work to seek after the truth in our midst. Still, it is a big step forward to be able to choose how you dress and what you wear and how you identify yourself gender-wise. We have certainly made some progress.

Your Story

Have you had experience with sex segregation in religious or other communities? Did it work well for you? What challenges did you find?

Episode 5—Balance as a Spiritual Practice

Let me come at this another way: God is *not* a man—and God is *not* a woman. God is *both* and *neither*. God has a feminine side and feminine attributes as well as a masculine side and masculine attributes. I have been blessed to be able to embrace both God's maleness and God's femaleness—and even God's in-between-ness. I see these as important conversations for spiritual communities to have. Not only *can* we find a balance between those two options; balancing those "opposites" is an important spiritual practice.

This is a place where we can learn from and appreciate the indigenous traditions and nature-oriented traditions that lean toward female gods and fairies and other feminine forms of divinity. We do not always have to stress the warrior God on the battlefield. God is also filled with gentleness and kindness and compassion and giving birth. In my journey, I want to combine these attributes within myself, so I might be a both or a neither who embraces all of who I am.

I am a man, but I have transcended the dualism of maleness and femaleness. I have gone beyond that crap, and I believe that it makes me a better man! I think that we need more trans men—not men who have just physically or mentally transitioned, but trans men who have spiritually transitioned. We can and we must also transform our spiritual selves into something more balanced.

I am a two-sided coin. Really, we all are, regardless of our birth history or gender identity. I have learned to flip it either way. I can shift my identity without feeling insecure about it. I continue to adjust and readjust—especially as I learn from my non-binary family. I have been watching them grow and learning from them. Oh, how they have blessed and nurtured me! They help me to be a stronger, better, more sensitive man!

I am thankful for the opportunities that I have found in spiritual communities where I have been accepted—not only for who I am, but also for who I am still becoming. As I navigate through the world as a transgender man as a part of these wonderful communities, each one of us looks at being transgender from a different point of view. We get to learn from one another in so many ways. Gender is not everything, but it is part of what we get to explore together as we worship God in spirit and in truth.

Your Story

Are there parts of your life where you have struggled to find balance? How have other people helped or challenged that process?

Chapter 5

Still Black

In addition to my journey into Judaism and through gender, I have also searched for spiritual connection around my Blackness. When I started, my *shul* only had two Black Jews—me and another guy. Every now and then, this other guy would show up. So, once every two or three months, there would be a total of three Black guys (and no African-American women) in *shul*.

I was happy enough with Judaism as a spiritual tradition and practice, but I set out on another journey—to find out more about what it meant to be a Black Jew. It took me to some surprising places!

Episode 1—Rasta(farian)s

Rastafarians are in some ways more known for their music than for their religion. Many do not know much about what they believe. It is an Abrahamic religious tradition (like Judaism, Christianity, and Islam) that developed in Jamaica. Rastafarians typically believe in Jesus (placing them generally among Christians). They believe that His Majesty, Haile Selassie, from Ethiopia was the reincarnation of Jesus Christ. However, they also identify strongly as God's chosen people, which places them in a complicated relationship with mainstream Judaism. Meanwhile, Rastafarians are very Afro-centric and organize themselves in a much more decentralized fashion—more akin to indigenous communities in Africa and elsewhere than to the institutional life of either Judaism or Christianity. While many lump Rastas and Rastafarians together, there are two different traditions with some diversity of thought and practice. For instance, Rastafarians eat meat while avoiding pork and shellfish, but Rastas are vegetarians.

I reached out to some Rastafarian Jews, but I found that they were quite prejudiced against what they called light-skinned Jews (Jews of European descent). I told them straight up, that I was married to a light-skinned Jew, so, they did not want anything to do with me. Later, I met another Rastafarian group that was not quite as hostile, but they still were not as friendly as I would like. I understand that Rastafarians developed their perspective in response to British colonial rule in Jamaica, but it was not an approach that was going to work for me. I was caught betwixt and between again.

Your Story

Have you ever felt like you had to choose between one part of yourself (or your community) and another?

Episode 2—Hebrew Israelites

I kept searching. I met Capers C. Funnye, Jr., who is a rabbi in Chicago, Illinois. He is a prominent leader in the (Black) Hebrew Israelite movement and heads up the International Israelite Board of Rabbis. Rabbi Funnye was the first African-American member of the Chicago Board of Rabbis and serves as a prominent bridge between the (Black) Hebrew Israelite movement and other (predominantly white) Jewish American groups.

Hebrew Israelite communities tend to be fiercely independent and sometimes even at odds with American Judaism—to the point that many in the Hebrew Israelite movement do not want to be referred to as "Jews" at all. Fundamentally, they make the claim that the African roots of the Hebrew Israelite tradition(s) predate the Judaism practiced in predominantly white synagogues. To be called a "Jew" may be insulting to someone who identifies as a Hebrew Israelite.

Rabbi Funnye is notable, not just as a "first" in terms of Black Jewish leadership, but also because he is a recognized leader who bridges both of these worlds. His personal mission is to unite all Black Jews together, whether they are in the U.S., Africa, or somewhere else. His motto is "A Jew is a Jew," but his method is to introduce all to Rabbinical Judaism.

In any case, I soon learned that there are Jews of color all around the world—not to mention Caucasian Jews who are raising children of African descent as Jews. There are Black Orthodox Jews and Black Reformed Jews and Black Jews in every denomination of Judaism. There is even a place called the Village of Peace (affiliated with the Hebrew Israelite movement) in the State of Israel, where Black Jews can go to stay while they work to gain citizenship. I was accustomed to navigating predominantly white spaces, but it was wonderful to realize that I was not alone as a Black Jew.

Your Story

Have you ever struggled to find people who "look like" or identify as you do? What did or would it mean to you to realize that you are not as much of a lonely exception as you once thought you were?

Episode 3—Strength for the Journey

Some of our enslaved ancestors from Africa were practicing Judaism before they came to North America—just as other Africans were practicing Islam or Christianity or African traditional religions before they were captured. Enslaved African Americans were the first "melting pot" as diverse traditions were forced together in the slave quarters. I like to imagine powerful interfaith conversations among those first arrivals, as Jews, Christians, Muslims, and traditionalists worked together under horrifically dehumanizing conditions.

Of course, they must have drawn strength from whatever traditions they brought with them from Africa. Black peoples have a long legacy of adapting to situations that might seem awkward. There is a certain kind of creativity that comes with needing to make a way out of no way, and I embrace all of the unexpected edges that I have inherited from my ancestors.

As Black folk, we have had to struggle together for generations, placing our need for survival above petty theological differences. I was raised to understand that what I did affected the whole Black community. Sure, we may squabble, but there is a practical kind of unity that comes from being a part of a marginalized group. If I stole something from the store, typically the Caucasian store owner did not say, "Oh, he came in here and stole a candy." He would more likely say, "Them Black folks ain't nuthin but thieves."

Jews have had similar experiences in terms of prejudice over many generations. These dynamics shape our culture and communities in many ways. As a result, Jews and Blacks have always had a lot in common in our struggles. We developed strong community and family values that we hold dear. These are some of the things that made it easy for me to get involved in the Jewish faith.

These many years later, I know many Jews of color. Some are gay or lesbian Jews of color. Some are scholarly Jews of color. I have met quite a few Black trans men who have chosen Judaism. I even have a friend who is in rabbinical school. He is the first Black transgender rabbi to be trained in the Reconstructionist movement.

Your Story

Have you ever experienced people who treat you like an oxymoron, even though your life makes good sense to you? How has your life's journey helped you to realize just how many impossibilities actually can exist, if you take the time to look?

Episode 4—Back to My Roots

As my search continued, I learned that the principles and concepts behind the laws in Judaism originally come from Africa. The Kemet people dwelt in the part of Africa we now call Egypt. The 42 Laws of Maat are believed to have been written down at least 2,000 years before the Ten Commandments of Moses. There are also reasons to believe that the Babylonian Talmud in Jewish tradition developed with significant influences from India.

Once I realized that Judaism itself was built on influences from ancient Egyptians/Africans and Indians/South Asians, it really expanded my mind and broadened my search. I learned about how the Jewish texts were gathered together over time. They were not delivered in the straightforward manner that I had imagined. In fact, the Jewish "Bible" was not canonized until 200 years before or after Jesus. The collection that we now call the Christian Bible was canonized even later.

The more I studied, the more was revealed to me. I wanted to find the story behind the story, the scripture behind the scripture, and the text behind the text. I wondered where all of this began. I came to understand that the Hebrew people gathered myths and reworked stories, as all people have done through the centuries, in order to fit the needs of a particular group of people and the society that they were trying to build. I finally came to understand that the stories of Judaism and Christianity and Islam were all allegories that were never meant to be read literally.

Your Story

Where have you looked to understand the beginning of things? What makes the sources that you hold dear feel more authoritative than others?

Episode 5—Both/And

Judaism strengthened my Christianity. It has made me a stronger Black man—and a stronger Black transgender man. Judaism helped me become a better person who is more productive in both Black and transgender communities. I continue to walk simultaneously with one foot in Judaism and one in Christianity because I cannot separate one from the other.

How could I say that Christianity hasn't shaped me? How could I say that my being a Jew doesn't matter? Even the Black pride I absorbed through the Nation of Islam has a deep, lingering impact on how I move through the world. Like my ancestors before me, I have combined multiple traditions through my own faith journey. I have survived by drawing on the resources I could find nearby (or sometimes after much searching). It has taken creativity to bring all of those influences together, over and against those who expect me to choose one way or the other.

At this point, I study sacred text like a Jew, but I emphasize anointing and incarnation like a Christian. I am loud, Black, and proud, but my spiritual life leads me to embrace the unity of all humanity—like Malcolm. While these juxtapositions may surprise others, there are no conflicts within me about how they relate to one another. I am a seeker who is searching for deeper truths, beyond the surface of such things. I am someone who is able to focus on shared values without being worried about petty theological differences.

Your Story

What resources have you looked to for sustenance on your journey? Are there some resources or opportunities that you did not have access to? Are there some resources that you had to search for? Are there ways that you still want to work to bring balance and peace within yourself about traditions that others may say are in conflict?

Chapter 6

Listening to Non-believers

As I continued to search for understanding and truth, I wanted to leave no stone unturned. Having considered all three Abrahamic traditions (and then some), I spent about six months considering the testimonies of non-believers. I connected with pantheists, atheists, agnostics, skeptics, humanists, and other non-believers.

These conversations raised new questions for me! Is God in everything? Is everything in God? What is this God—and is this God real? Is God a part of nature? Is nature a part of God? What is really going on with all of this God-talk?

Episode 1—More Bibles

Being a good preacher, I started out reading *The Atheist Bible: An Illustrious Collection of Irreverent Thoughts* (2007) by Joan Konner. This anthology is divided up into chapters and books like you have in a religious Bible. However, the content highlights writings from atheists and other non-believers. To my great surprise, many of these readings resonated deeply with me!

For instance, the Book of Thomas (Paine) begins, "I do not believe in the creed professed by the Jewish Church, by the Roman Church, by the Greek Church, by the Turkish Church, by the Protestant Church, nor by any church that I know of. My own mind is my own church" (*The Atheist Bible*, Chapter 23).

The Book of Mark (Twain) begins, "Faith is believing what you know ain't so" (*The Atheist Bible*, Chapter 20). I rather thought that was right—and a challenge. Is it okay to profess what I know is not true?

This quote from John Keats also struck me: "My Imagination is a Monastery and I am its Monk" (*The Atheist Bible*, Chapter 17). If my journey into African perspectives led me to question the authority of ancient texts, this phase led me to question religion more broadly.

I went on to read *The Satanic Bible* (1966) by Anton Szandor Lavey. Neither *The Atheist Bible* nor *The Satanic Bible* is considered sacred text in the way that the Christian Bible is for Christians. They are certainly not revered by followers as is the Torah. However, *The Satanic Bible* remains influential.

Far from the flagrant blasphemy that I expected, *The Satanic Bible* is actually a thoughtful examination of religious belief. I suppose it is important to clarify that "Satan" in the Satanic Bible is more of a metaphor for personal liberty and individualism than the antagonist imagined in other religious traditions. Instead, the external religious ideas ("God") are placed in tension with human nature and strident libertarianism ("Satan").

So, to summarize, Satanists teach that human nature has been attacked recklessly and without reservation by all of these ideas about God. Instead, Satanism invites us to embrace our "lower" selves, to embrace self-interest and greed as something positive, basically to take every religious dogma you can imagine and turn it upside down. Satanism lifts up indulgence, vitality, and even vengeance, in contrast to religious traditions that emphasize abstinence, sacrifice, and self-denial for some greater good.

These critiques of Christianity really got me thinking! They made me want to be a better human. I began to think about exactly what it is that makes people ethical. I really don't think it is a belief in God. Being a non-believer has nothing to do with your character or with how you treat other human beings. It has to do only with your beliefs and how you worship.

It quickly became clear to me that these non-believers had a strong belief system of their own—and a lot of energy to pursue it! In an atheistic worldview, there is no God, which is a very equalizing approach. In other words, none of us is more divine than the other. Additionally, there is no evil greater than that which lies within each of us.

Your Story

Have you ever taken the time to really consider those who disagree with you? Why or why not?

Episode 2—Freedom from Religion

During that six months of exploration, I also was reading Richard Dawson, Christopher Hitchens, Richard Gere, and other prominent non-believers who were challenging church doctrines. I even went to a conference hosted by Freedom from Religion, an organization dedicated to the fact that there is no God—and they had so much literature! The conference gathered atheists from across the country. They had buttons and t-shirts, books, and everything you can imagine! There were workshops, and people even shared their testimonies about how confident they were that there is no God.

Freedom from Religion also works with pastors who left their pulpits and started life all over again as atheists. They recognize that many pastors want to leave the church, but they cannot do it because they only have two or three years left until retirement. They do not want to risk losing their pension. Moreover, some clergy have no other means to make a living, because, when they went to seminary, they were not learning other transferable skills. It is easy for me to imagine how hard it would be to stand in the pulpit, Sunday after Sunday, preaching about something I no longer believe.

So, Freedom from Religion offers practical support and job training for former pastors. Whether someone is a religious leader or not, Freedom from Religion recognizes that it is a huge shift to leave Christendom. They help people adjust—to losing a congregation, to losing friends, to maybe even losing a spouse or family or kinship network. In this way, coming out as atheist has a lot of similarities to coming out as gay. Sometimes, people become very isolated when they are abandoned by their entire support system.

Atheism is treated as something very shameful in much of the world. In so many ways, it is treated like a dirty secret. Your whole life may be turned upside down if you leave God behind. It is often more acceptable to change religions—to change to a different Abrahamic faith or even to another tradition that is widely recognized such as Buddhism. To say that God does not exist is somehow considered a most terrible sin. So, at this conference, people were sharing testimonies about how they survived—and about how free they felt after leaving all of that behind.

Your Story

What do you believe about non-believers?

Episode 3—Non-believing Faithful

When I was converting to Judaism, our class was invited to a Jewish man's home for discussion and sharing. He was a Holocaust survivor, and he said he had become an atheist because of his experiences during that time. Even though he no longer believed in God, he was one of the most observant Jews that I knew. He put lots of effort into Jewish community, working with the youth, teaching about our heritage, even though he did not believe in God.

We asked him, "If you don't believe in God, why are you still laying *tefillin*? Why do you still go to *shul*? Why do you study Torah?"

He said it had nothing to do with God. It was only because the teachings of the Torah and the Jewish people are his heritage. He said the law was of the people and not from this "so-called" God. He believed that they are helpful rules designed to help the Jewish people maintain order and gain strength.

I learned that you can be deep in your faith—whether that is Jewish or Christian or something else—and not believe in God. As I

33

listened to non-believers, I still wondered, if you don't believe in God, then why spend so much energy on convincing people of *nothing*? It does not exist. It is not there. So, why are you spending all this money, all this energy, all this time to say, "God is nothing?" But, it is clearly something that is very important to them.

Your Story

Is God the only reason you seek to live an ethical life? What other motivations might someone have for living an ethical or moral life?

Episode 4—Black Non-believers

There are Black atheists and Black agnostics and Black humanists and Black seculars. They, too, had transitioned away from belief in the Christian churches. For them, it was not just a religious question but also a question of how Africans and African Americans have been treated under the banner of religion. Let me tell you, there is a lot of dissatisfaction with the Christian church!

> As my ancestors are free from slavery,
> I am free from the slavery of religion.

Thelma "Butterfly" McQueen

Even though I was not ready to be an evangelist for non-believers, I did resonate with the freedom that they offered. I was particularly taken by this quote from Thelma "Butterfly" McQueen (an actress who had a role in *Gone with the Wind*). She was also a devout atheist her entire life.

This quote has stuck with me in so many ways. By this point in my journey, I did feel free from religion and religious dogma, but I did not feel free from a belief in Creator God. So, I began to wonder more about whether these might be two different things—being free from religion or being free from God.

Still, after that season of exploration, I just knew that I could never settle for the God of the Christian tradition ever again. My Jesus is bigger and greater and more expansive than what I had ever been offered by Christians. I could never go back.

Your Story

Have you ever had such a turning point in your own life? Have you ever reached a point of no return where you knew you could never "go back," no matter what the cost?

Chapter 7

My Religion Is Love

My spiritual journey and search for the truth about God has continued into what people call Hinduism. The guru who led me in this direction is called Amma, and Her mantra is "My Religion Is Love." Unfortunately, there has been much misinformation about this tradition in the West, so let me back up a bit and explain some of what I learned.

Episode 1—Finding Amma

It is often said, "When the student is ready, the teacher will appear." This is certainly true of my journey. In reality though, my shift toward Hindu religion started when I fell in love with a woman named Triptta. Triptta was living in a California *ashram* when we met and I began to be involved in her community, not as a seeker, but as her boyfriend—to be near her. Triptta's *ashram* follows the teachings of Mātā Amritānandamayī Devī, who is called "Amma" for short.

In the beginning, I would go to the *ashram* to visit Triptta. I would sit and listen. I would enjoy the music and watch the dance of the bright lights in the fire. Amma is called the "hugging saint." I would go to Her programs and get a hug from Her. I read Amma's books and would visit with Her each year when She traveled to our area. I also listened to those who had been taught by Her.

However, through all of this, I was not looking for a guru! Like many Christians, I was raised to look down on Hindu religion for various reasons. For one, having a guru seemed like blasphemy. You have to listen to your guru and obey your guru. I thought that a guru was to be worshiped instead of God—but that was my misunderstanding. There are different ideas about gurus in different traditions in terms of beliefs about how they gain their power and insight, but, in the end, a guru is revered and respected simply because they are a spiritual leader or guide to others. It is not more complicated than that.

I do not bow to my guru because She is God. I bow to my guru because we are all connected—because we are all One. I appreciate this sense of connection, not only to other humans, but to animals, plants, and even inanimate objects. I understand that every person, place, and thing is a manifestation of the One Supreme Being who is our source. This is something that I found much more clearly expressed in Hinduism than I had in other traditions.

Amma teaches that She is like "the finger pointed at the moon. [She is] not the moon itself." In other words, She does not pretend to be God. She guides others and does what She can to make the world a better place. Any great Hindu guru would have a similar teaching. So, this was not the big conflict I was expecting it to be as I learned more.

Your Story

Have you ever had a teacher or spiritual guide who really helped you find your way?

Episode 2—One God

The true or original name of the Hindu faith is "*Sanatana Dharma*," which translates into English as the "eternal truth" or the "eternal religion." With no known founding figure, *Sanatana Dharma* has diverse, but ancient roots. It is considered the oldest major religion still being practiced today. There are several written texts to draw from, but teaching emphasizes guidance from the gurus even more than from books.

"Hindu" is actually a term that refers to the Indian subcontinent, to a geographic location, even though several other religious traditions also emerged from that region. "Hindu" became a shorthand for *Santana Dharma* in the 19th century C.E. and has gained traction since then, even on the subcontinent. Beyond the cultural diaspora of continental India, *Santana Dharma* is typically not understood very well. In fact, Amma and Her *ashrams* are my only long-term experiences with Hindu teaching—and that is only possible because Amma travels to the United States regularly.

I grew up believing that Hinduism had many gods. Some say there are 33,000,000 gods in the Hindu faith! However, the actual teaching is that *Krishna* is the Supreme Being and the source of all existence. The rest of the 33,000,000 are understood to be different manifestations of *Krishna*. Like the many names for God in Abrahamic traditions, the many aspects of *Krishna* are more than our limited human minds can hold at one time. For me, this clarification was a critical step in opening me up to the wisdom of my new teachers.

36

Your Story

There is so much misinformation in the world. Are there any people or traditions that you might like to hear from first-hand instead of by rumor?

Episode 3—Purpose

Eastern traditions (for example, Hindu, Buddhist, Jain) tend to be organized around alleviating suffering, repairing the world, and finding our way home. Each tradition and each path has a particular way of talking about these themes, but there is none of the "heaven" or "hell" business that is espoused in Christianity and even Islam. There is no "us" and "them." In Hindu tradition, each of us works toward peace within ourselves and in the world around us, but there is no deadline for achieving "perfection." As an "eternal path," the Hindu framework does not have that sense of urgency about being "right."

Santana Dharma is a way of life even more than a religion. It is a worldview and a framework for understanding everything. We do not recruit or proselytize because this is a non-dualistic point of view. We understand that all of the things that seem to separate us are only illusions. They are not truth. Bowing to one another and talking about Oneness helps us to see that everything that exists has emanated from the Divine, even if there are surface elements that seem to separate us.

For instance, Amma will never ask someone to give up their other religious beliefs or practices. I get to bring my Jesus and my Judaism and everything else that I have brought with me on this journey. All are welcome to the *Santana Dharma*, regardless of mental or physical condition. We are in this together!

Your Story

How might your approach to life change if you stopped worrying about being "right" or "wrong" and simply embraced the process?

Episode 4—Three Paths

There are three paths in *Santana Dharma*. *Karma yoga* is the path of action. This is a physical path of selfless service. *Jnana yoga* is the path of knowledge. This is the path of intellect and self-realization. *Bhakti yoga* is the path of loving devotion to a personal god. The personal god varies with the devotee. This is the emotional path.

While the Western world typically thinks of "yoga" as a kind of semi-spiritual exercise, "yoga" actually means "union" (in Sanskrit) and these are all paths to union. The three paths are not mutually exclusive—

and you do not choose one path over and against the others. Rather, they are three different ways of expressing commitment and growth. The relative emphasis on *Karma yoga*, *Jnana yoga*, or *Bhakti yoga* will vary with each individual practitioner. Each person gets to find their own comfort zone in terms of how they express themselves.

I love the way this approach accommodates different kinds of people with diverse personalities. The Hindu faith does not elevate selfless service above self-realization. Neither are devotional practices elevated above the others. Each path is useful and each of us is encouraged to pursue the practices that we need most to find balance and peace in our own lives.

Your Story

Have you ever felt pressured to follow a path that did not feel "right" for you? Can you imagine shaping a path that was custom-made for your own temperament and needs?

Episode 5—Seeing Is Believing

For me, seeing is believing. I like to "people watch." What really drew me in and put the icing on the cake for me was watching Amma's presence and impact. I learned about the ways She feeds thousands of people and watched her minister to people, sitting for as much as 18 or 20 hours at a time—just sitting there hugging people and listening to what they have to say. She gets treated like a rock star, but I have also seen her sweep floors and clean and do common stuff in her white sari right alongside her people. She makes an example of herself.

She is a true humanitarian, and the power of her work has moved me deeply. She builds hospitals, nursing homes, and schools. She provides aid in times of disaster (for example, Hurricane Katrina). She does not provide this support just for Hindus or Buddhists. She provides it for human beings, regardless. In twenty years, I have never even heard a rumor of her taking a day off—even for a sick day. She is tireless about working to stop suffering in every way.

Amma gave me a mantra and, after She knew me for several years, She gave me my Hindu spiritual name, which is *Subodh*. It means "one who knows his true self." She has helped me to treat everyone and everything with more reverence. We are all connected. Indeed, love is the only true religion—and love is shown by selfless service, giving of oneself and of one's time and energy for others.

Your Story

Who are the people you trust the most in terms of their life's work? What kind of people have you seen really making a difference in the lives of others?

Chapter 8

Cultivating Quiet

One of the things I noticed and wrestled with as I moved from tradition to tradition had to do with how we practice, reflect, and communicate with and about the Divine. There are so many ways to be in the various traditions. Some are more contemplative. Some are more intellectual. Some are more emotional and physical. Frankly, some work for me and some don't!

Episode 1—Christian Diversities, Race, and Culture

I was once in a local church group where we would have centering meditation twice a week. The gathering was based on Psalm 46:10, which says: "Be still and know I am God." The whole endeavor was influenced by the writings and teachings of Thomas Merton. The facilitator would lead in with this phrase, but then repeat it—shortening it by a word each time through:

> Be still and know I am God.
> Be still and know I am.
> Be still and know.
> Be still.
> Be.

We would then silently meditate on these words. Our focus moved to the quiet in each one of us. We would each be focused entirely on being with God by just being—not by doing or saying or singing. In addition to being a way to relax, this practice also reminded us that we are human *beings* who are *being* with God in every moment just because we *are*. This helps us remember being-ness instead of busy-ness. After a silent walking meditation in a circle, we would join hands and walk forward toward the candle and silently bow to the light.

However, this shift was really hard for me, coming from African-American, Pentecostal, Baptist, and Black church backgrounds. We were not very big on moments of silence when I was growing up. Sometimes movies and such will exaggerate what our worship is actually about without understanding it, but, beyond the caricature, there is some truth to it. We do place a lot of emphasis on singing and dancing—and even shouting and carrying on. Of course, there are historical reasons for this, and your mileage will vary as some traditions are significantly more energetic than others.

Sometimes, we think we are talking about religion, when we are actually running headlong into issues of race, class, culture, nationality, and historical circumstance. Many people forget that enslaved people were not allowed to read. In fact, it was illegal to teach a slave to read. So, many of the patterns of community engagement among African-Americans emphasize call and response between the congregation and a leader in ways that do not require widespread access to books, paper, or even literacy. These patterns are also connected to our roots in Africa, which predate the written word or modern educational standards.

Instead of thinking of African-American worship as having an *emphasis* on emotional or physical experience (which varies), I like to think of it as not making an idol out of the written word. Now, Black folk will *talk* plenty about "the Word"—and gaining access to literacy and educational opportunities is something that our communities tend to value quite highly. It is just that after our communities have been denied access in so many ways, it does not make sense for us to organize our gatherings in ways that exclude those who can't read. In other words, several generations of oppression have helped us to remember that we do not need paper resources to worship God together.

The call-and-response style also frees us up to be more interactive, because we don't have our noses down looking at some piece of paper. The interactive dynamic helps the community to be more connected. A stronger feeling of oneness can develop between the leader and the community in such a setting. Even when we read the Bible or sing in worship, there is often repetition. First of all, repetition makes it easier to catch on to what is happening, making it easier to participate. The song leader may also "line out" the words so that the congregation can join in singing verses without looking at hymnal or bulletin. Even scripture might also be doubled as it is read by a reader and then repeated by the preacher as a way of teaching and reinforcing the text.

Seeking the stillness of *being* with God through practices such as contemplative prayer impacts our brains. It is not just a mental or spiritual practice, but it also changes the chemicals in our brains. So, too, high praise, that is, energetic worship, also has a physical impact. Our brains are wired to release endorphins to ease our pain and give us extra energy. So, our praise has spiritual, psychological, and even chemical benefits—which are a literal balm in Gilead, a healing practice in communities that endure great pain.

Your Story

Do you expect religious expression to be a quiet observance? Or an active engagement? Which are you most comfortable with?

Episode 2—Jewish Commentary

Meanwhile, the idea of debate and questioning is something that I learned from Jews and Judaism. You just question, question, question—and you debate everything! There's a standard joke among Jews: "You ask two Jews one question and you get five different answers."

When you are studying the *Talmud*, you find lots of different opinions about the Torah text and the other issues at hand. Everybody gets to put in their version of what they think the text really means. In Jewish tradition, all of these interpretations are considered valid. There is an understanding that we are continuing to write the Torah every day, that we are keeping it fresh, because more things are being revealed every day.

That practice is modeled for us in the *Talmud*. Each time a question is asked, you will have five or six different rabbis answering the question and giving their commentary. You get to read the different opinions and wrestle with it for yourself before you decide what makes the most sense to you—and there is still space in the tradition to add your own interpretation. Obviously, not everyone's opinion gets added to the *Talmud*, but there is a lot of freedom around the idea that your opinion really matters.

So, in Jewish community, we can sit at a table, and we can go back and forth over what this rabbi and that rabbi said. We can even debate about the men who wrote these commentaries (and they were *all* men). So, you can read and read and read—and then you get to contemplate and meditate. As I said in chapter 2, there are also the *Mishna* and the *Zohar* and the *Tanya* and the writings of Maimonides. You get to see what the great rabbis and great sages had to say through the centuries.

I find it all really exciting. I could sit for hours and hours to consume page after page and book after book. This approach really suits the way I like to search and explore. I suppose that I just extended my searching, reading, and arguing beyond the Jewish texts. So, I take that Jewish approach to scripture and commentary into my reading of Christian and Muslim and Buddhist and Hindu texts as well.

Your Story

How do you feel about discussions such as these, without a final resolution? Have you been taught to look for a single, final, absolute answer? Or do you have experience with a more multi-vocal approach that honors a diversity of opinion and interpretation?

Episode 3—Silent Retreat

All the Eastern traditions (including Buddhism, Jainism, Hinduism, and more) tell us to "Go within." I enjoy going to an annual eight-day silent retreat in Hawaii that is led by Amma's North American *swami*. It is fabulous. For eight days, the only person talking was the *swami*, who is the leader of the retreat. We would be in a group of people sitting, meditating, having meals, going for walks, but no one else was saying a word. We were in total silence for most of the day.

After that length of time, you really kind of get used to it. At the end of the eight days, there is a debrief time where we gathered together to discuss the experience. We sat in a circle and everybody introduced themselves. People kept saying, "I've been with you for eight days, and I didn't even know what your name was!" We were together, but we did not know what each other's voices sounded like. Still, there was a sense of connection and togetherness even in that silence. Even after it was over, we found ourselves walking around the campus and still not speaking to each other. It had become a habit and a different way of feeling connected and sharing space.

Not only was no one talking, but we were also not supposed to be on Facebook or the internet. We were taking a break from the world. It's actually like Shabbat in Jewish tradition, where from Friday night to Saturday afternoon, you don't watch TV or go on the internet or do anything like that. You take a break and rest from all of that busyness. It's a day of silence. Some people call it a fast because we are abstaining from electronics—an electronics fast.

For many of us, this is a huge challenge. Could you give up your phone for a whole day? Can you stop checking your email? Stop checking your Facebook, Twitter, and Instagram? Can you give up reading the newspaper? Would you be willing to unplug for a few days?

Most people are so busy that it is hard to imagine taking a break for even just three hours, let alone three days. However, even taking a one-hour break can help to clear the mind. Shut the computer down. Turn your phone off. Even just 20 years ago, we did not have computers and phones like this—attached to us 24 hours a day, seven days a week. We can survive without it! We will be better for having the break from constant stimulation.

Meditation can also be physical—whether that is doing a yoga pose or a relaxing stretch. When we were at the retreat, every day twice a day, we had a walking meditation where we went for a walk. We would meditate as we walked—watching the waves, looking closely at the sand, or taking off our shoes to let our feet sink into the grass.

There were grounding exercises that helped us get that connection with the energy of the Earth. In the quiet, it can also be easier to reconnect with nature and our bodies. Whenever I stop and take a deep, relaxing breath, I feel the flow of the energy run through me. I let my body relax and take a moment to get my thoughts together. I've learned to be quiet before I speak. It helps to just slow down.

Your Story

How do you feel about letting go of the busyness of life? Are you at ease in silence? Are you comfortable drawing your attention to just *being* in your mind, in your body, or in your spirit?

Episode 4—Buddhism and the Monkey Mind

When most people enter into a time of silence—for one minute or eight days—our minds go all over the place. That is normal. I used to think there was something wrong with me. I was in a yoga class or in a meditation class. I thought I just couldn't meditate, because everybody else seemed to be "in the zone." People would laugh at me because I was telling them that I could not do it!

It was easy to imagine everyone else had some peaceful serenity that I was missing when I was sitting in a room full of people who looked quiet, but you don't know! I might be thinking about Donald Duck on TV when I was six years old—and you would not know it! You cannot see or assume what is going on in someone else's mind just because they are sitting there with their eyes closed, their back straight, their legs folded, and their hands in a peaceful gesture.

When I began to meditate, my mind was all over the place every time. The Buddhists call it the "monkey mind." Your mind goes every which way, and you cannot concentrate. I learned from great teachers to just sit there and be quiet. The trick is to stop worrying about whatever it is that is running through your mind. I am learning to let those thoughts come and then let them go.

The first step is to take the time to sit and be still. That is the first step to meditation. I am not a visual person. I do *not* like guided meditation. If it works for you, then that is great for you, but you can't guide me anywhere! When I close my eyes, there are no birds in the air, no ocean waves, no sun rays coming down on me, no balloons rising up. I guess my brain just does not work for that kind of visualization. In any case, guided meditation does not work for me, and I have talked to lots of people for whom it does not work.

But, I do know that that you can sit there every day—maybe just

45

for one minute a day. Can you be still for one minute? Do not try for 250 hours or even 53 minutes. Can you just sit there for one minute? For some people, sitting still for 60 seconds is a hard thing to do—but you do it. Every day, you do one minute. Then, you will get to five minutes. Then, ten minutes. The next thing you know you are up to 20 minutes, to 30 minutes, to an hour—but it takes time and practice.

Even then, you still cannot keep your mind quiet. Nobody can. Meditation is not my strongest point, but I have gotten much better as I continue to practice. Sometimes, I just count backwards from one hundred to zero while I sit there. I have found that helpful to still the voices in my head.

Your Story

Have you encountered your own "monkey mind"? What is your experience with guided meditation, mindfulness exercises, or contemplative prayer? What is your relationship with silence like?

Episode 5—Speech is Silver. Silence is Golden.

The practice of going within is not just something that comes from Eastern traditions, though it is something that I really appreciate about Eastern traditions—and it is something that has kept me coming back to the Hindu approach. Indeed, I have found myself growing through these practices much more than I had in the meditation and prayer practices of other traditions, where I was praying on my knees, bowed down, trying to get a word through to the divine. Cultivating quiet feels more authentic to me than striving to feel something that *sometimes* just isn't there. Now, I just work on relaxing into the quiet.

It is common in Hindu communities to meditate with mantras and chanting. For me, that just does not work. However, working to clear my mind in my own ways remains an important part of my practice. I have to work to keep my mind organized and focused. With my mind in good order, I am better able to move in the world. That is what the Hindus have taught me, even though everything they do does not work for me. I appreciate that there is still space for me in their communities.

Overall, I think that many of us are afraid of being silent. Often, we take refuge in meaningless talk and laughter, which reveals that so many of us cannot endure the thought of being left alone with nothing to do. That is why we spend so much time with TVs, radios, Facebook, and all the rest. We are afraid to be alone.

I have seen this proverb, "Speech is silver. Silence is golden." I like how it lifts up silence. However, if you read it closely, you will also see it saying that speech is valuable. I am a voracious reader. I love African-

American church traditions that involve music and movement. I also love Torah study. Cultivating quiet is another part of my practice that helps me find balance. You don't have to do it the same way that I do it or the same way that others do it.

Your Story

What might it be like for you to try to quiet your mind for 60 seconds? To take a walk by yourself in nature? To pick a day to be silent at home with your partner for the day? What works best for you to center yourself and keep your mind clear?

Chapter 9

A World of Wonders

The truth is that there is often more than one thing happening at any given time. So, while I am trying to tell my story in an orderly way, there have been many layers of experience—sometimes happening simultaneously. So, let me back up and fill in some of those gaps with a few more layers.

Episode 1—Riding with CC

CC was my "ride or die." She was a butch dyke way back in the 1970s. I met her on her motorcycle with her sleeves rolled up. I was just starting to crossdress and figure out where I might fit in. CC taught me about drinking and "reefer" and playing craps. My mom called her a "hoodlum," but I loved her. She was my best friend and we were together trying to find our way in a world that did not much care for our well-being.

CC had a hard time getting jobs because of how she was in the world. This was in Newport News, Virginia, in the 1970s! We could not even get into a lot of bars because of how we were. I got CC a job washing dishes, but we both lost our jobs after she kept coming in late to work. We washed cars for a while. We sold heroin for a while. Eventually, I got a job in a hospital, and CC got a job doing billing for a construction company. We ran with a small group of folk and we took care of each other as best we could.

Sometimes, CC turned tricks. It turns out a lesbian can make good money with men. Somehow, they think it is cool to try to "turn" somebody. Well, CC got pregnant from one of her tricks. It was hard enough getting by and she already had one little boy to take care of on top of her lady friends. For lack of money, she went for a backroom abortion with a coat hanger. Something went wrong, and she bled to death on the table.

I would go out on Saturday night and still show up to Baptist church Sunday morning, but CC would not have anything to do with putting on a dress and trying to fit in like that. CC was raised Roman Catholic and had believed everything they told her. She was convinced she was going to hell for all the things she had done.

When she died, it was more grief than I had ever known before. It was all I could do to go to the funeral home to view the body. They put lipstick on her and got her into a dress. I had *never* seen her like that, and I knew that this was the last thing in the world that she would have wanted. It broke my heart. The group we ran with fell apart once she was gone, so I felt very alone.

Now, growing up Baptist, I did not have anything good to say about the Roman Catholic faith. However, I was so devastated about CC's eternal fate that I found my way into conversation with a Roman Catholic priest. He told me all about purgatory. So, I started working with the goal of trying to get CC out of purgatory. I would have done anything to keep CC out of hell. I wanted her out bad. It meant everything to me.

So, I started taking catechism classes and attending Mass. I was on my way to rescue my friend! I was fasting and praying and repenting. The more I went to class, the more I was unhappy with it. I could not shake this depression that had come over me.

In the midst of that depression, I wandered into our favorite bar and had some Purple Haze with Nehi Grape Soda. Next thing I knew, CC walked into the bar. We talked and walked. We found a place to watch people going in and out of bars. We talked for hours. Eventually, I had to go to the bathroom and CC laughed at me, saying, "We don't have bathrooms where I am."

I said, "I am hungry."

She said, "We don't eat food, either."

I was tempted to stay right there with her, but we made our way back to my girlfriend's house. Obviously, I was tripping, but I did not know that at the time! My girlfriend let us in and put us to bed. Cee Cee was gone by the morning, but I was still tripping. My girlfriend went for a long walk with me because I was determined to go find Cee Cee. We must have walked 15 miles before I had come down again from that high—and I was hungry, so we would stop at every restaurant or fast food joint on the way.

Eventually, I came back to myself. I went back to the Catholic church, looking for consolation. This time, the priest told me a thing or two about how *I* was going to hell, too. So much for comfort. After that, I left the Roman Catholic Church for good. I have met other Catholics, including some Black Catholics, along the way. So, I know there is more to the Catholic tradition than what I experienced at that time. However, that was a formative experience for me and made it hard for me to explore the tradition in later years.

Your Story

Have you had any traumatic experiences that have haunted you? Are there representatives of certain traditions that wounded you so deeply that you just can't go back?

Episode 2—Pagan Friends

Years ago, I had a therapist. Actually, she was one of the best therapists that I ever had before I moved to California! I was seeing her as a gender therapist in order to get access to hormones or surgery or other medical interventions. In addition to being a therapist, it turns out that she was also a witch who was involved in a Wiccan coven.

Now, growing up Christian, I had heard all kinds of horrible things about Wicca, witchcraft, and other kinds of Pagan practices. This was 1992 and I was still involved with the Christian fundamentalists. My friends knew my therapist was a Pagan and they were warning me that she was a devil—a dangerous, evil woman who would corrupt me.

Still, I appreciated the conversations that we were having in therapy, and I liked her style. It was therapy, so we talked about everything, including my faith journey. I was interested in her story, too. Over a couple of years of working together, she had some opportunities to explain a little about her Wiccan practices, including why she had chosen that tradition, especially as a woman.

Her coven would host events at the changing of seasons. She encouraged me to attend a harvest ceremony to find out what it was like. There was fire and I love the fire! There was also dancing and camaraderie, but it was a woman's coven and I was already on this journey to affirming my manhood! So, that just did not seem like a good fit.

Now, I was not generally hanging out with my therapist, because that would not have been appropriate. However, I met one warlock—that is, a male witch—and he became a mentor of sorts. He introduced me to a secret bookstore, where you could buy things for spells and potions. If you knew how to ask, you could access the Church of Satan through the door and into the basement. So, I attended a Black Mass and watched and listened and came back to some of their events at different times.

At one point, I was considering making a love potion to deal with a situation in my own life. The potion promised to have this girl falling head over heels for me! However, in the end, I did not go ahead with it. I knew that was not going to be "real" love. If the potion would have worked, it would have only been my controlling or manipulating someone else—and that is not what I was actually after.

What I learned from that season in my life is that you cannot believe everything that someone may say about another person's religion.

Any practice or tradition can be used to manipulate or cause harm. I knew that from my own experience in Christianity, too. There is black magic and white magic, but Pagan traditions are not inherently bad. Pagan practices can be used for good things or bad things—just like anything else. One of the most important things about spiritual practice is cultivating your own intentions and how you use the power that you have.

I also had experience with a number of different traditional religions (including African indigenous traditions). I saw them get worked up so that their deities would mount them—or they would channel spirits. I struggled some with those experiences because there was enough smoking and bourbon and whiskey involved in some of these gatherings that it was not good for my own recovery. However, I was touched by my experiences being with them, and I do not regret having studied with them at all. None of these Pagan communities was the dangerous rabbit hole that my Christian siblings told me that they would be.

Your Story

Have others "warned" you about certain traditions? Have you ever explored a tradition that someone else had warned you about? How did that turn out?

Episode 3—Called to Ministry

When I was excommunicated from the fundamentalist church, it broke my heart. I mean I was cold—just frozen. All my other feelings disappeared into this unbelievable pain. I wanted nothing to do with the church or with religion.

MCC brought me back and gave me space to heal. I started studying for the ministry with them. In my fire for outreach ministry, I started a support group that eventually added a Bible study component. I had this dream about building a recovery center where people could rebuild their lives with community and spiritual support. At that time, I was also finding Black theology and theologians such as James Cone. We were teaching African Heritage in this Norfolk community center. This was my African awakening period.

With all this going on, the pastor of First African Baptist church reached out to me and was encouraging me to grow my ministry for people who were unchurched, who had mental health or emotional issues, or who had substance abuse issues. I was ordained under that pastor, but, soon, it got complicated. It turns out he was just using me.

My group was for transgender and gay people—and anyone who was unchurched, suffered from mental health challenges or substance abuse. I later learned that this pastor had told the National Baptist

Conference that *he* was ministering to gays and lesbians, but that the goal was conversion. Of course, I had already been through an ex-gay ministry and I was not about to bring that kind of harm to my people.

So, that was a huge disappointment. I felt like I had set my people up—like I had led lambs to the slaughter. Their hearts were broken when they heard about all this—and they wanted to "lay hands" on somebody about it (not in a good way). Well, I convinced them that making a fight out of it would only make matters worse. I had a good job, so I was O.K. financially. I would clock in and clock out, but I sunk into a depression. I felt that I had been robbed of my purpose. Well, one day I came home from work to find eight people sitting at my dining room table. These were my people—and they had gotten themselves together to come and ask me to be their pastor.

They said, "We love you and we love the church." They said, "We want to have our own church—a church where nobody's going to put us out." They said, "We want you to be our pastor." Well, of course, I was deeply moved and could not say no to their pleas. I did not want them to be left bitter from the experience. That is how I became the pastor and founder of By the Way Baptist Church in Virginia.

I loved those people and I did my best, but it became clear that I really was not qualified (yet). So, after three years I realized I was over my head and needed formal education. I decided that I needed to leave them so I could learn how to be a better pastor. I moved to California where I attended Pacific School of Religion, was ordained at City of Refuge UCC (as a part of the Fellowship of Affirming Ministries), and also became a certified substance abuse counselor.

I felt like all of that education and certification was important preparation for my ministry. I wanted to lead a church where you could come to the altar and get more than just prayer. I wanted to be able to help people take those next steps in recovery, too.

Your Story

Have you ever struggled with a call to ministry? Have you ever felt unprepared to do the work that needed to be done in your community? Have you ever been asked to serve anyway?

Episode 4—Jewish Jesus and Beyond

I did not leave my Christianity behind as I moved into my Judaism. I brought pieces with me and incorporated everything into one as I grew. I was grateful to be able to bring Jesus with me—and not to have to deal any more with all of the baggage that goes along with the blood, the cross, the crucifixion, and the resurrection in so much of Christian tradition. Jews do

53

not believe that Jesus was the Messiah or the Christ. They do not believe that Jesus came to save or deliver or anything like that, but they still believe that Jesus was a rabbi, a teacher, and a healer.

In other words, according to Jewish tradition, if Jesus was the Messiah he would have brought peace, become a ruler, and set up a kingdom here on earth. The Temple in Jerusalem would be fully restored. The kingdom of heaven would have come, and there would be peace on earth. That is the work of the Messiah. Since Jesus did not do all of that, Jews do not believe that Jesus was the Messiah—and that was all right with me.

Jesus and I still have a great relationship, but not *that* type of relationship. I walked with Jesus into Judaism and I understand him to be my first rabbi. There are books that helped me with that journey back. For instance, I would recommend *Walking in the Dust of Rabbi Jesus: How the Jewish Words of Jesus Can Change Your Life* by Lois Tverberg.

Jesus told me about Judaism because he was a Jew. I follow Jesus on the way into Judaism. But, I am also following Jesus all the way to India. I found my Jesus was really getting around—and the places I followed him did not always leave me compatible with other known branches of Christianity at all.

I had to move on to another Christianity. I had to find another right road. I had to build my own religion, my own holidays, my own traditions, and strike out on my own.

Your Story

Have you ever tried to reimagine traditions in which you have been involved?

Episode 5—Church for the Fellowship of All Peoples

I was a Jew and a free-thinker and a Black Hebrew Israelite. I was still involved in City of Refuge UCC—and I also spent some time at the Church for the Fellowship of All Peoples which was co-founded by Howard Thurman. This was a super-inclusive church that was built to be interracial and interfaith from the very beginning. So, I would go to synagogue on Friday night and Saturday morning. Then I would go to Church for the Fellowship of All Peoples at 11 a.m. on Sunday. Finally, I would land over at City of Refuge for 1 p.m. service.

The Church for the Fellowship of All Peoples had a lot going for it. It was both educational and mystical. The service was meditative. The conversation about whatever we were reading was intellectual. We shared meals in the fellowship hall after the service. It was like being a part of a really thoughtful family.

Unlike many of my other family-church experiences, this was a family that celebrated indigenous people. It celebrated a variety of different religious traditions. It celebrated people of all different skin tones and ethnic backgrounds. Unfortunately, it was a small church with a very limited outreach ministry. I was still eager to roll up my sleeves and work with the marginalized. Otherwise, the Church for the Fellowship of All Peoples would have been a pretty good fit for me.

Your Story

Have you ever tried to find peace by adding more and more commitments to your life? How did that work for you?

Chapter 10

Finding Freedom

Even after I adopted Amma as my guru, I was still doing a lot of reading. I learned about Jiddu Krishnamurti, who turned my life upside down! My perspective got changed and rearranged—for the better.

Episode 1—Non-dualism

Jiddu Krishnamurti was groomed for leadership by the Theosophical Society from a young age. When the time came for him to take leadership, he proclaimed that he had nothing to teach. Still, he went on to write many books, and you can even find his videos on YouTube—but his main teaching was that you do not need a guru, you do not need a church, and you do not need to go to Temple. You just need to look within for your own truth.

Krishnamurti's teaching focuses on non-dualism—that is, the idea that there is no separation between things that we normally think of as separate. In other words, we are all connected. Krishnamurti argues that the separation we so often talk about is violence:

> When you call yourself an Indian or a Muslim or a Christian or a European, or anything else, you are being violent. Do you see why it is violent? Because you are separating yourself from the rest of mankind. When you separate yourself by belief, by nationality, by tradition, it breeds violence. (J. Krishnamurti in *Freedom from the Known*)

Coming at this from a different angle, God is the only thing there is. There is nothing else but God. We are all God. Everything is God. God is in everything. The only thing that is *is* God. You cannot separate yourself from God. It is just not possible to get away from God.

If God is everything, then everything is God—the night and the day, the light and the dark. They are not actually different things. They are more like two sides of the same coin, but it is all God. This teaching means that sickness and health, life and death, too, are a part of God. No matter what it is or how it feels, it is still part of God. So, there is no "Satan" and no "devil." In fact, there is no "other" at all. There is only the idea of separation and the reality of oneness.

Now, we are dualistic people who live in a dualistic world. We have to use our five senses to maneuver through the world. But, beginning with Krishnamurti, I began this journey toward non-dualism and not separating myself. Non-dualism is a central theme in all of the Eastern traditions, and it has changed my entire life, including my theology and how I move through the world. This approach is the freedom that I was looking for all along. Indeed, it offered me the freedom to rebuild my whole point of view.

Your Story

What has your relationship with dualism and separation been?

Episode 2—Big Changes

At this point in my journey, some things really had to change. It was like going into an old demolished building to salvage old bricks or other construction materials for something new. I had to sort through the old materials, pick and choose what seemed worthwhile, and then clean them up. That's what my process was like.

I went into each tradition and grabbed some bricks that seemed useful for my new path. I had to re-examine each and every one of the things that I had been taught all my life. I had to let go of some old teachings to make space for newer ideas and ways of being in the world. The chapters in this book represent some of that process of rebuilding.

Number one on the list of things I re-examined was my idea of God. Who and what is this God about whom we are always talking? Where did this God come from? What does God want? Where does "he" live? And what does he have to do with some of the problematic things that I had experienced?

Humans were created with an instinct to know—to search and find out where we came from. Some religions like to say we came with all the information we needed, but we lost it somehow (through "the Fall" or "sin" or something like that). I rather believe that this eternal knowledge was written on our souls in invisible ink. Society and all sorts of different people start adding their clutter onto our souls as soon as we are born, so that we often forget the important insights that still live underneath all of that mess. It is our job to pull away that clutter to find our original insights, written in the deepest part of our true selves.

Of course, many of us accept what we are taught as children. Children of Christians become Christians. Children of Jews become Jews. Children of Muslims become Muslims. We are told that we are boys when we are born, so we grow to become men. We are told that we are girls when we are born, so we grow to become women. There is a lot of pressure to accept what our families and communities tell us about ourselves and the world.

However, questioning what we have been taught is an important step toward the kind of freedom that I am talking about. We need to learn how to challenge those teachings and how they operate, even within ourselves. There are layers and layers of exploration and rebuilding for each one of us in order to find the eternal knowledge that is our first inheritance and birthright.

I began to look at it as developing a path to reach the God within *me*—not a faith for you or for my partner or for the lady down the street, but a faith that is for *me*. I don't get to decide what *your* faith needs to be. Your faith is a very personal experience. I began developing a faith that was just for *me*.

Non-dualistic religion means having the ability to accommodate anything and everything, because each of us has different needs and experiences. All religions show us how to develop compassion, love, faith, forbearance, and endurance. This is basic and central to my faith. I carry Amma's saying with me: "My religion is Love."

Now, you may be wondering how I can reconcile this Oneness with people who cause harm, but let's not get lost in the details. My point is that we cannot even begin to understand the infinite power of the Divine— deep and wide and embracing of all that is. As you have read in these pages, I have experienced plenty of abuse that I would not wish on anyone. What I am saying is that God is bigger than all of those things that I have experienced.

Your Story

What if the Divine really is *within* you? What teachings have you received that may need to be reconsidered?

Episode 3—Rethinking God

Among all of my other studies, I also read about the science and psychology of God. Scientists have looked at the chemistry, the DNA, and the neural activity associated with religious activity. There is a place in our brains that is built for God! Our brains create God and our image of God. It is something that we all have as humans. This does not diminish God. In fact, it reinforces the idea that God is an integral part of what it means to be human.

Sorting through all of these different traditions, I have heard: "God is in you" and "God is in heaven" and "God is on earth." Well, where in the world is God, really? Either God is too big to be contained in the universe—or maybe our experience of God is in our brains and follows our gaze everywhere we look. Everywhere we go, we find God—because God is *in* our brains. It might be that God is a chemical reaction, or it could be that an "out there" external God wired us to connect with them through that part of our brains. Either way, I believe that God is in our brains.

This leads me to the conviction that belief really does matter, because everything is energy. Everything has a vibration and is a part of the whole—even and especially the thoughts in our brains. Mantras and chanting work (for some people) because the repetition has an impact on our brains. There is a rhythm to the energy that is being released. Similarly, our intentions when we say prayers or spells have an impact on our brains. Some brains are wired with the need to express themselves more physically, emotionally, and spiritually, even though others are less so. That diversity of temperament is born into us even before we get inundated with the cultural norms and expectations that surround us.

Processing all of this, I started to laugh a bit at myself (and so many others) trying to study God. It has consumed many hours and days and years of my life! Both religious devotees and atheists have spent a great deal of time on it, but in the end, we still don't know—and maybe that is a good thing! Isn't it better to accept that we don't know than not to realize it and keep arguing?! What if it is O.K. not to know? What if it's not about finding the right book or teacher? What if we will never find a perfect explanation for the *everything* that we are already a part of?

Let me say that again. We are already a part of God. I love the idea that God is revealing God's self through you and through me. Indeed, God is experiencing the universe as you, through you (and as me, through me). That is what being one with God or being one with the universe means. We are the incarnation of God here on earth.

Your Story

How do you react to Jonathon's suggestion that we center our understanding of God within the human brain? How would you describe the God of *your* understanding?

Episode 4—Circles and Cycles

The idea of reincarnation is perhaps one of the most widely known aspects of Hindu religion. Everything goes around and around. We see it in nature, when leaves fall off of trees and grow back again or when flowers seem to die off entirely, only to return the next spring. The seasons teach us about how life comes and goes and comes again.

I also think it is important to connect the teaching about reincarnation to the Oneness that I have been talking about in this chapter.

Reincarnation is not so much a lonely, eternal wandering, longing for closure. Rather, it is about belief in a circular and cyclical life, in the way that all things are connected through God.

In fact, I've written this book with something of that spirit. Our conversation has not moved from beginning to end. Rather, we have circled and cycled back through themes and seasons in my life. I realized that I could not fit everything about one topic in one straightforward chapter. Instead, I am spiraling through. I am telling you about different seasons of my life, then returning to that topic later so I can go deeper into some aspect of it the next time around.

Similarly, I have faith that I don't have to work everything out in one lifetime, any more than I have to share everything that can be said in just one chapter. There is no hurry because I will get another shot at this the next time around! My past lives inform my experience now. In this lifetime, I will learn new things to take with me for the next one. In the midst of this, God is being born and reborn into the world through each one of us.

Your Story

Have you ever had to revisit themes and challenges you faced earlier in your life? How did those experiences deepen your understanding?

Episode 5—Rethinking Ethics

Some might say that teachings about reincarnation remove the threats of "heaven" and "hell" and therefore also remove our motivation to be ethical creatures in *this* lifetime. Indeed, much of what religion offers is an ethical framework through which we can engage the world. However, we do not need God or the threat of violence to be ethical creatures!

Non-dualism has helped me to reorganize my ethics around love and relationship, rather than rules or some threat of eternal violence. A fear-based religion, that is, one that is based on threats, is a means to control people. In that way, religion can function like a fascist government or a schoolyard bully—and that is nothing to be proud of. Even if the expressed goals are the same (for example, compassion, love, community), getting there by way of threats and violence makes no sense.

Instead, non-dualism teaches that we are all connected, so threatening others to get our way is only doing harm to ourselves. If there is no separation, then doing violence to others is doing violence to ourselves. Instead, I want to pay attention to how we are all connected.

Religion should not be focused on preserving a tradition or power or control. So, Krishnamurti really helped me to sort this out. Now, I realize that I do not need a church or a synagogue or a mosque or a temple or a guru. I have learned a lot through churches and synagogues and Amma and all the rest of my explorations. So, I am not saying that these traditions or things are useless. However, I do not *need* any of them to be a spiritual or ethical person.

No one has the right to claim that their religion is superior to others. Of course, many people really object to this. They say, "My way is the right way, and, if you don't do it my way, then you will never find peace." In the end, I believe that fighting each other in the name of religion is not conducive to bringing peace into the world. It is really that simple.

I want to be a living Bible, a living Torah scroll, a living testimony. I want to be a light in the world like Jesus, like a Shabbat candle, like the fires that burn away the ego in Hindu tradition. By looking within, it is easier for me to stop worrying about what everyone else is doing.

I want to live and work and be in community. I stay connected to Amma's organization because they are a group of ethical people who are doing selfless service in the world. I like having the opportunity to be a part of their humanitarian efforts—and I like being in community with like-minded people.

I live in an *ashram*. An *ashram* is a Hindu spiritual community, similar to a monastery, a Buddhist temple, or another residential religious community. People come to an *ashram* when they want to work on their spiritual practices—to go within. The quiet of an *ashram* means that there's less to take your mind away from your spiritual practices. Of course, this is 2020, so we do have the internet. We do not live in complete isolation (global pandemics notwithstanding). However, we limit how much time we spend on electronic entertainment.

In the *ashram*, we are trying to focus ourselves on growing spiritually. We provide services and care for others, including the animals and the earth. There are gardeners and animal keepers and accountants at an *ashram*. We do all of these things (and more) to the glory of God. If I am watering flowers and I understand that the flower is God, then I am caring for God. If I am feeding a cow and I understand that the cow is God, then I am feeding God. If I give a cup of soup to a hungry person and I understand that person is God, then I am doing it not just for God but to God and with God.

Your Story

What kinds of motivations inform your ethics? Do you try to be a "good" person because you are afraid of something "bad"? Or are you motivated by connection, relationship, and love?

Episode 6—Finding Freedom

For me, freedom means being a Christian who believes that Christ is reincarnated over and over again in this world, in me and in you. It means being a Jew who is an independent thinker, who does not believe in Jesus as Messiah or even in God, but who does care about my community. Freedom means clearing away the clutter that has been laid on my spirit to find my own eternal truth within me, without fears about "heaven" and "hell."

For me, freedom means letting each person find their own path—recognizing that my path might not work so well for other people. Meanwhile, I am learning to replace the illusion of our separation with love and connection. Freedom means leaning into that oneness with other people, but also with the trees and the sheep and the stones and even the bugs. We are all a part of the universal plan. Nothing comes from nothing. Everything is a part of something. We are all a part of the whole of our religious experiences.

I believe that we are all manifestations of the Divine. We are all more than the image of God, because we are a part of God. In this freedom, I also believe that we create God and that God is evolving together with us. We are co-creators who are repairing the world together. We are helpers to the universe. We all have our role in it, working on behalf of God.

Freedom also means that I am continuing to seek and explore and grow spiritually. My DNA test told me that I am descended from the Igbo people in what we now call Nigeria, so I am learning about where and who I come from. Freedom means acknowledging that I do not have all the answers, but also that I do not *need* to have all of the answers.

Your Story

What does freedom mean to you?

Afterword

Finding Another Right Road Authentically and Holistically

I hope that you have enjoyed this journey through my trials and tribulations, my explorations and insights. My road has not always been easy, but it has been worthwhile.

My current ministry is called **Trans Anointing** (www.transanointing.com). It is designed to support people of transgender experience, trans expressions, and those who have transcended gender boundaries in realizing our own sanctification (being set apart) and consecration (dedication). Obviously, this book project is a part of Trans Anointing and one way that I am sharing from my experience.

Before Trans Anointing, I was already talking about **Finding Another Right Road Authentically and Holistically (FARRAH)**—which is not trans or gender specific. The FARRAH approach is for *anyone* who is exploring their spirituality and seeking spiritual independence. It is for those who need a spiritual or religious alternative, for those who are willing to bring their own oil to the anointing and sanctifying of one's own body as a place of worship, and for those who are living out our own truth in the universe as our true Divine selves.

Building and Rebuilding

In the pages of this book, I have described some of my process toward developing my own spiritual path and religious perspective. I picked up a brick from Christianity, a brick from Judaism, a brick from Hinduism. We could argue about where each of these bricks came from and how they are "supposed" to fit together, but I do not worry much about those questions any more. I began to stack my bricks all together as I was led by spirit—and now I have a shelter for myself, with enough doors and windows to let the light in. The Spirit of God holds my bricks together, in these new constructions and that is good enough for me.

In my building and rebuilding process, I am looking at each religion and comparing it with all the other religions that I have practiced, read about, or otherwise experienced. If I find something that is a theme or practice in at least three traditions, then I am going to make a special note to myself about that. For instance, every religion that I know of encourages prayer, meditation, or incantations. Many talk about renunciation and fasting. The Oneness of God is a common belief. Not causing harm is an important ethic that we find in many traditions and it has led me to become a vegan. Selfless service is a part of most traditions.

Choosing Bricks with Discernment

As I have demonstrated through these many episodes of my life, just because a theme or practice is widespread does not mean it will come easy to me. I was frustrated by several different kinds of prayer and meditation. However, I kept exploring and trying new things. For me, cultivating quiet in combination with grounding exercises is particularly useful, but the more structured meditations of chanting, mantra, contemplative prayer, or guided meditation do not work well. You might have a different experience! A good general rule is that you should not force yourself to do things that are not enhancing your spiritual growth. Every thing is not for every one.

I believe that renunciation is about transcending dualism—and that is why it is found in so many traditions. Fasting is about being *in* the world, but not *of* it. Sometimes, it is about cultivating quiet, or trying to do less harm with our lives. I do not believe in denying myself just to *create* suffering. That does not feel right to me. However, abstaining from certain things can help me to restore balance, rebuild connection, and overcome separation. It can be a part of removing all of that built-up clutter that I have allowed others to place upon me, so that I can seek out my inner truth beyond the many illusions of this world.

While many traditions have sacred text, it is not essential that you focus there. For me, reading is really fun and exciting. I have learned that Christians read their texts differently than Jews who read their texts differently than Hindus. Personally, I spent too much time worrying about all of those different details for a long time. Of course, I still read a lot! But, now, I consider all of the stories in these sacred books as allegories and myths and parables. They can be useful as long as I do not get too caught up in them. Remember, they are religious texts, not history books or science books.

Similarly with traditions, I may celebrate Christmas on December 25, but that does not mean that I believe Jesus was *actually* born on December 25. Many of our most familiar traditions have been influenced by *other* traditions. For instance, some traditions are simply seasonal events that get packaged within the stories of each tradition: mid-winter and new year traditions, spring traditions, and harvest traditions.

The metaphor of seeking the light within you is a common theme in many religions, even though it might be expressed in different ways. I love fire, so this is another theme that really works for me. You might resonate more with images of water or air (wind and breath) or the earth itself. These are images that transcend traditions, also. You may resonate with planting seeds and tending to the growth of plants. You may even resonate with particular animals or with the way the planets and stars influence our lives—but it may be something else that suits you better and rings true in a deeper way for you. Work with the medicine that works for you!

It is not so different with people. I have shared about some of the mishaps that I had looking for mentors—call it what you want: guru, pastor, rabbi, imam, teacher. Now, I really watch the way people conduct themselves. Someone's behavior speaks volumes about who and how they are. I don't want you to tell me that you're a good Hindu or a good Muslim or a good Christian. Let me see you love someone. Let me see how you love everybody. Let me see how you love people who are less fortunate than you and have "nothing" to offer. I want to see how you show respect and care. I want to see if you are serving selflessly. I want to know if you will go out of your way to help others.

When I find people that meet these kinds of criteria, it usually shines like a light pouring out of them. I can see that their spiritual practice, whatever it is, is real because of how it empowers them to be in the world. They believe in whatever they believe in, and they live that life—maybe with teaching, maybe with singing, maybe with dancing, maybe with contemplation or prayer. When I find people living out loud like that, I find it inspiring regardless of what tradition they may represent. If they can do it, then maybe I can, too. So, those are the people that I want to listen to and learn from. I am less excited to spend time around people who tell you one thing but actually live in a different way than their words would suggest.

Growing in Spirit

Who is the God of your understanding? Is it a person? Is it energy, consciousness, sub-consciousness, super-consciousness, or called by many names? Finding Another Right Road means growing beyond religion and control, hate and malice for those who may believe something different from you. How you relate to the God of your understanding is totally up to you. Your path will lead you.

I do not care whether you have a BIG God or a little God or if you think God is a bad influence. Each of us has to develop our strength and abilities, like a baby eagle learning to fly. We have to learn to fly, too. If we never get out the nest to try something new, we are not going to grow. We need to get out and experiment. We need to do our own due diligence in figuring out what is real and what is only illusion. Our five senses may betray us sometimes, but it is still important to balance engaging with the world and looking within.

Each of us has scars, literal and figurative, that shape us. Some may be obvious to others. Some may be hidden deep in our inner life. Growing spiritually does not mean wallowing in that pain, but it does mean taking our pain seriously. We are microcosms of the universe, so tending to our own pain is also tending to the pain of the world. Do not let anyone tell you that it is selfish to take care of yourself. It may be important to touch your pain to claim your story and sort out the ways that it has shaped you, but it is also important to put the past behind us and learn to live in the present moment.

Whatever words or practices you use, if love is your religion, then we are family. We do not a God to love one another. We do not need a God to control us with some promises about heaven or hell. Hopefully, the God of your understanding is someone who helps you to embrace your own insights and experiences. Whether you are a Christian or a Muslim or a Buddhist or a Pagan or an agnostic or atheist or something else, we can still be family in love. You can reject all of those labels—or weave together more than one of them in your own way. As Louis Mitchell likes to say, many of us are "Holy Hybrids."

FARRAH and Trans Anointing are about seeking spiritual independence. Worship is not about a building or an institution. It is about how we live out our truth in the universe. It is about the divinity that is within us, whether we are transcending gender boundaries or religious boundaries.

Our African ancestors in slavery did not have a choice about how to worship. They had to adapt to the many demands of their owners and may have adopted some toxic assumptions just to survive—but they were also creative and independent within the constraints of their time.

I have been a seeker for all of my life, but it has taken me a long time to get free. Now, I know that I do not have to choose. I do not have to stay in one place. I can go with the flow of the spirit in me. I can appreciate my siblings and their various practices. I can go to the full moon service. I can dance in the moon light or roll in the mud. I can worship God in all kinds of different forms and likenesses.

I have made this journey from Christendom to freedom. Because I am now free, I can visit a group and recognize when I am at peace with them and when I am not—without internal pressures and expectations. That's what I see as true freedom—when I can come and go as I please, when I don't have to be afraid. If I don't want to bow my head and pray, then I don't. If I don't want to chant, then I don't. If you asked me to lead prayer, I can decline or pass without guilt or shame.

At the same time, if you are in need and you need a blessing I feel empowered to do that for and with you. I can send you all the love and energy and hope and strength that I have in a way that is honest and truthful and unique to me. That is where this journey has led me.

I tell my story because I want you to know that you do not have to be stuck with the religion you were assigned at birth. You do not have to settle for the traditions that were handed to you by your family or the neighbors who came knocking at your door, either. Take the time to find the path that is right for you. Make something new that works for you. Don't get caught up in trying to choose just one tradition.

I love my trans siblings. The vast majority of Black trans folk have Christian origins. I have traveled through many of the great religious traditions of our world, from Mexico to India to Israel. None could give me all the answers that I was looking for or the freedom that I needed. Non-dualistic traditions invited me to look within in a different way. That helped me to recognize that I had a *responsibility* to bring something new into being.

I am not telling my story because you need to follow the same path as I have. I certainly wouldn't wish upon anyone some of the heartbreak that I have experienced. But, I do want other free-thinking and independent-thinking people to know that someone is listening.

Religion tried to kill the spirit within me—and if it were not for religion, I would not be here with a story to tell. To quote our ancestor Maya Angelou, I wouldn't take nothing for my journey. I can't go back. I don't want to go back. I have no desire to go back, but the weight has been lifted from my shoulders. Now I float in the sea of love, and where the waves take me is where I need to go.

The highest value is freedom. I am an atheist theist. For me they are one and the same. To me there is no difference. Now, that is freedom!

The Point of Religious Diversity

All religions share a common root, which is limitless compassion. They emphasize human improvement, love, respect for others, and compassion for the suffering of others. In so far as love is essential in every religion, we could say that love is a universal religion. But the various techniques and methods for developing love differ widely between the traditions. I don't think there could ever be just one single philosophy or one single religion. Since there are so many different types of people, with a range of tendencies and inclinations, it is quite fitting that there are differences between religions. And the fact that there are so many different descriptions of the religious path shows how rich religion is.

H. H. The XIV Dalai Lama

Works Cited (or Recommended) by Chapter

Preface

The phrase "God is still speaking" was popularized in an United Church of Christ advertising campaign.

Introduction

The opening quote in chapter 1 is from Thelma "Butterfly" McQueen quoted in the *Atlanta Journal and Constitution* on October 8, 1989. For more about McQueen, please review "'Gone with the Wind' Icon McQueen Was Lifelong Atheist" (July 14, 2019, with video) by Rick Snedeker at https://bit.ly/2QCghfG (Patheos.com).

The photo known as "The Scourged Back" is in the public domain, but attributed to McPherson & Oliver. For more about the story, please review "The Shocking Photo of 'Whipped Peter' That Made Slavery's Brutality Impossible to Deny" (February 7, 2019) by Erin Blakemore at https://bit.ly/3bmDcU6 (History.com). The photo accompanied the article, "A Typical Negro," which appeared in *Harper's Weekly* (July 4, 1863).

Beginning with Christianity

Scofield Reference Bible (1909 first edition). The *Christian Bible* is available variously in many English translations.

The Lord Is My Shepherd—and, He Knows I'm Gay: The Autobiography of the Reverend Troy D. Perry (1987) by Troy Perry

Where the Edge Gathers: Building a Community of Radical Inclusion (2005) by Yvette Flunder

OtherWise Christian: A Guidebook for Transgender Liberation (2019) by Mx Chris Paige

OtherWise Christian 2: Stories of Resistance (2020 anthology), edited by Mx Chris Paige

Converting to Judaism

For more about the Transcendence Gospel Choir, please review https://bit.ly/39dUFwH (Transfaith.info).

Jewish sacred texts (Torah, *Talmud, Mishna, Tanya, Zohar*) are available variously in English translation.

Balancing on the Mechitza: Transgender in Jewish Community (2010 anthology), edited by Noach Dzmura

Exploring Islam

The Qur'an is available variously in English translation.

The Autobiography of Malcolm X (1965) by Malcolm X with Alex Haley

The Muslim Alliance for Sexual and Gender Diversity includes stories from several transgender Muslims in their Azaan project at http://www.muslimalliance.org/azaan.

You can reach out to the Trans and Muslim Project through Transfaith (https://bit.ly/2WESrDO).

More on Gender

Womanist Midrash: A Reintroduction to the Women of the Torah and the Throne (2017) by Wilda Gafney

God and the Gay Christian: The Biblical Case in Support of Same-Sex Relationships (2015) by Matthew Vines

Still Black

Still Black: A Portrait of Black Transmen (documentary, 2008), http://www.stillblackfilm.org/

Black on Both Sides: A Racial History of Trans Identity (2017) by C. Riley Snorton

Black Trans Prayer Book (2020 anthology) edited by J Mase III and Dane Figueroa Edidi

Listening to Non-believers

The Atheist Bible: An Illustrious Collection of Irreverent Thoughts (2007) by Joan Konner

The Satanic Bible (1966) by Anton Szandor Lavey

Freedom from Religion Foundation, https://ffrf.org/

Gone with the Wind (1939 film)

Black Freethinkers: A History of African American Secularism (2019) by Christopher Cameron

Love Is My Religion

For more about Mātā Amritānandamayī Devī ("Amma"), please visit https://amma.org/.

Cultivating Quiet

New Seeds of Contemplation (1962) by Thomas Merton

Transcending: Trans Buddhist Voices (2019 anthology), edited by Kevin Manders and Elizabeth Marston

A World of Wonders

James Cone is credited with advancing Black liberation theology and published numerous books. Three early works of interest were *Black Theology and Black Power* (1969), *A Black Theology of Liberation* (1970), and *God of the Oppressed* (1975)

Pacific School of Religion, https://psr.edu/

Walking in the Dust of Rabbi Jesus: How the Jewish Words of Jesus Can Change Your Life (2012) by Lois Tverberg

Jesus and the Disinherited (1949) by Howard Thurman

Finding Freedom

Freedom from the Known (2009) by Jiddu Krishnamurti

Wouldn't Take Nothing for My Journey Now (1994) by Maya Angelou

Afterword

Trans Anointing, http://www.transanointing.com/

About the Author
Jonathon Thunderword

Jonathon Thunderword is a theologian, a scholar, and a free thinker. He is an omni-faith, multi-spiritual practitioner who is a part of Mata Amritanandamayi Center.

Jonathon is an ordained Christian minister, founder of Finding Another Right Road Authentically and Holistically (FARRAH) and founder of By the Way Ministry in Virginia. He is a certified Alcohol and Substance abuse counselor. He is also affiliated with National Alliance on Mental Illness (NAMI) Faith Network, Transfaith, TransSaints, The Fellowship of Affirming Ministries (TFAM), Pacific School of Religion (alumnus), Lehrhaus Judaica (Hebrew student), Black Trans Advocacy International, and Brothers Rising (Oakland, CA).

Jonathon has spent his adult career trying to relieve suffering—working with persons living with AIDS/HIV, homeless populations, people with addictive behaviors, sex abuse, spiritual/religious abuse, and those that are marginalized. He is also an environmentalist and an animal activist.

You can reach Jonathon Thunderword at
http://www.transanointing.com/.

More Resources from
OtherWise Engaged Publishing

OtherWise Christian: A Guidebook for Transgender Liberation
by Mx Chris Paige

OtherWise Christian 2: Stories of Resistance
edited by Mx Chris Paige

Christian Faith and Gender Identity:
An OtherWise Reflection Guide
by Mx Chris Paige

In Remembrance of Me, Bearing Witness to Transgender Tragedy:
An OtherWise Reflection Guide
by Mx Chris Paige

And more to come!
Please visit http://otherwiseengaged4u.wordpress.com
to learn more.

OtherWise Engaged Publishing

OtherWise Engaged Publishing is excited to be working with the best and brightest of OtherWise-gendered folk! We provide a multi-tradition, independent publishing operation for projects from OtherWise-gendered folk that are in alignment with our values.

Visit otherwiseengaged4u.wordpress.com
for information about our latest releases
and to support independent transgender-led publishing.

What are the words you do not yet have?
What do you need to say?
What are the tyrannies you swallow day by day
and attempt to make your own,
until you will sicken and die of them, still in silence.

Audre Lorde

YOUR NOTES (Chapter 1)

YOUR NOTES (Chapter 2)

YOUR NOTES (Chapter 3)

YOUR NOTES (Chapter 4)

YOUR NOTES (Chapter 5)

YOUR NOTES (Chapter 6)

YOUR NOTES (Chapter 7)

YOUR NOTES (Chapter 8)

YOUR NOTES (Chapter 9)

YOUR NOTES (Chapter 10)

www.ingramcontent.com/pod-product-compliance
Lightning Source LLC
Chambersburg PA
CBHW071601040426
42452CB00008B/1249